The
Whole
Counsel
of
God

" . . . for I did not shrink from declaring to you
the whole counsel of God." Acts 20:27

The Whole Counsel of God

by Carl E. Braaten

FORTRESS PRESS
PHILADELPHIA

Biblical quotations from the Revised Standard Version of the Bible,
copyrighted 1946 and 1952 by the Division of Christian Education
of the National Council of the Churches of Christ in the United
States of America, are used by permission.

Library of Congress Catalog Card Number

ISBN 0-8006-1064-4

4057173 Printed in U.S.A. 1-1064

To

T. F. Braaten

K. F. Braaten

O. F. Braaten

C. S. Braaten

A. F. Braaten

F. M. Braaten

C. A. Braaten

All preachers and missionaries —

May their tribe increase!

Contents

Part Four

THE WHOLE MAN

Preface

This collection of sermons spans the past six years of my preaching, both in seminary chapels and sundry congregations. The themes that I have been working on in my theological books are grounded here in the medium of preaching. I happen to believe that "preaching is where it's at." Theology has no higher calling than to make straight the way for preaching the gospel of Jesus Christ. It has been my intention — the success of which is not for me to judge — to make my theology and preaching keep an eye on each other. Neither should be up to something the other cannot understand or approve.

Ever since I was made to think about preaching — and how could I avoid it with a father as a preacher — I found that two ideas were hardening into immutable convictions. The first is that preaching, just because it is conveying the Word of God, can only be done in "fear and trembling." That has stayed with me, but it is not visible on the surface. It is felt as a deep suffering in the inner man. The second is that the preacher dare not preach anything less than "the whole counsel of God." Obviously, the two convictions go together. If a sermon were just an editorial, there would be nothing to fear, no reason to tremble. But "the whole counsel of God" — who is equal to the task?

I am working with the theme of the "whole" throughout these sermons. But I cannot claim with the apostle Paul that I have declared here or anywhere else "the whole counsel of God." That is for me, perhaps also for Paul, an eschatological notion. After all, it was he who said that now our knowledge is partial but in the end it will be whole (1 Cor. 13:12). Yet, we are committed to the vision of the whole — our hope and our goal.

The imprint of Luther and the heritage of the Reformation have left the strongest mark on my preaching. Their battle cry for the *totus Christus* and the *totus homo* have not been mere fighting slogans of sixteenth-century polemics, but positive symbols of a theology of the gospel that challenges us to explore more deeply the realities to which they point under the very new conditions of twentieth-century life. This theme of the whole has also animated our ecumenical vision; but, as the sermons show, we will not settle for a cheap edition of catholicity at the expense of the truth and priority of the gospel. Authentic ecumenism must seek the wholeness of the church via the true proclamation of the gospel. It is my hope that we may be found to be in faithful continuity with the best in our past, without repeating it, and at the same time in vigorous contact with the issues of our time, without conforming to it. For preaching, like theology itself, must move in tension between the pole of our apostolic identity in Christ and the pole of our engagement in the concrete world.

Chicago, Illinois   Carl E. Braaten
July 1, 1973

Part One

The Whole Christ

1

The Trip
that Jesus
Took

Isa. 53:5 "But he was wounded for our transgressions, he was bruised for our iniquities; upon him was
the chastisement that made us whole, and with his
stripes we are healed."

One summer evening I accompanied a group of pastors to a
park in Tacoma, Washington. We went because we heard the
Jesus-people were there for a week of evening rallies. It was
everything we had been led to expect — long hair and hip
clothes, freaky looks and rock music, youth evangelists
moving around with Bible in hand, asking people if they are
saved and ready for the second coming, pointing to Scripture
passages to prove what they believed. We heard a lot of
Jesus-talk, "turning on to Jesus; it's out of sight; it's a beautiful trip." We heard personal testimonies of how people had
dropped out of the straight culture of living at home, going
to school, getting a job, and choosing a career, and then
getting into drugs and sex, dodging police, sitting in jail,
getting terribly sick, until the day they met the Lord and quit
their flesh trips. They called it the "Jesus trip."

The Jesus-people get very excited. They talk about what
has happened to them, how they have changed, how once
they were like this but now are totally different. It is very
zealous, personal, and hypersubjective. That is not so much

3

the style of most of us. The Jesus trip can mean two things. It can mean the trip *you* are taking — what is happening to you, how you are feeling about Jesus inside, where you got saved, when it happened, how much you wish others would be as happy as you. Then you are talking about your Jesus trip.

Then there is the trip Jesus took — very sobering! — what happened to him, why he was killed, who ganged up on him, and, above all, where is the good news in the catastrophe of his death. Our style is not so much to make *our* trip the important thing. The Gospel is the story of Jesus' trip. Classical dogmatics referred to it as the "work of Christ," or as the doctrine of atonement. Especially in Lent, leading up to Good Friday and Easter, we go over the ground again, tracing out the trip that Jesus took. It was a bloody trip — a bad trip — blows and burdens along the way.

What is the meaning of his trip? Every age interprets it in its own categories. The theologians of the ancient church had an interesting idea. They said that God sent Jesus on this trip as a ransom to the devil, in exchange for the captive human race. The devil gladly accepted the ransom, and let the people go. The devil took hold of Jesus, but in killing him went too far, and thus lost his claim on both Jesus and the human race. In this way all mankind was led back to God by the trip that Jesus took. The devil was tricked and fooled.

Here you have the picture of two superpowers negotiating for the human race, its peace and salvation. It is like modern diplomacy, the Nixon trip to China, toying with the fate of millions of people who have nothing to say about the outcome. We would hardly interpret the trip of Jesus in such a way today.

About a thousand years later another theory came along, worked out by Anselm of Canterbury. He looked on the trip of Jesus into the jaws of death as the price God demands to free the people from the death penalty. Man has sinned and hurt the honor of God. Like a feudal lord God requires some payment, some real satisfaction, to offset the sins of mankind, by someone as good and innocent as all the rest are sinful and guilty. Jesus was such a man, because he was divine and sinless. This is what Anselm heard in the words, "He was wounded for our transgressions, and he was bruised for our iniquities." Again, today we would hardly find in our own culture the images to see Jesus as a sacrifice for sin, as a payment God requires to satisfy the formal demands of justice. We would not say these views are wrong; only that they are of another day and age, of another culture and experience.

We can look at the trip of Jesus in still another way. Jesus was caught up in the personal, social, and political transactions that concern everyman. There is no escape. He was wounded and bruised, he was despised and rejected, he was made full of sorrow and grief, he was smitten and afflicted. Our sins caused it. That means the sins of all of us together — not my petty personal sins and foibles as such, but the whole system of human solidarity of which I am a part, the whole network of human relations, every sphere, every office, every group, every power, every job, every knowledge — all of it together became a trap, a conspiratorial plot to suck a person into that same system, to break him and make him knuckle under, to cut him down to our size, to refuse to let him be the exception he was. Organized forces and institutions of evil to which we are linked in every personal act landed upon Jesus. Jesus grappled with evil and the sources of evil, and they snapped back at him, bruising, wounding, and slaying. But he remained obedient to the Father, faithful to the kingdom he preached.

It has been common in the evangelical tradition to stress that it is our personal and private sins that put Jesus to death. We like to dwell on our own personal sins; it makes us feel important. We like to slosh around in our personal feelings, good or bad. But Jesus took a trip into public places, out in the open where worldly forces collide. There are public forces and public works of evil and public sins. Jesus was exposed to them all in public and he died a public death before all who had eyes to see. We have tended to spiritualize this event, as though his trip is essentially into our souls, as though he is snooping around on the inside, peeking into our private feelings and poking around into our dirty thoughts. That makes each one of us feel so important, making the smallest pygmy look like some mystical giant. But Jesus first took a trip into public places. Why make this real history an allegory of a mystical trip that a person can take by psycho-analysis or personal introspection? Perhaps there is a time and place for that too. But Jesus' trip was into real public places, and he really got blasted by public forces. We will deal with some of them.

The organized religion of the chief priests and the religious leaders of the people put Jesus to death. It was their religious zeal and bigotry. They were angry with Jesus. He flaunted the Sabbath, broke the laws of fasting, ate forbidden food, and with people who did not wash their hands to boot. This same zeal showed itself in the inquisition and in both ancient and modern religious wars, Catholics and Protestants in Ireland killing each other, Moslems and Hindus in Bangladesh killing each other, Buddhists, Catholics, and Communists in Vietnam killing each other, Greeks and Turks in Cyprus killing each other. This public power of religious bigotry, this spirit of the inquisition, is not a thing of the past. Jesus was put to death by that power at work in human history. Many times since, religious leaders who have called themselves followers of Jesus would have put him to death the same way the chief priests and elders of the people did then.

There were other public forces. There was graft and bribery. Money had a hand in it. The people who controlled the concessions around the temple were the same ones who paid off Judas. Their business suffered the day Jesus chased the merchants away from inside the temple gates. Blood money put Jesus to death. It is the same blood money that runs Chicago and other big cities; it is graft and greed. We read about it in the papers; and what they tell us, as bad as it is, is perhaps only the visible tip of the iceberg.

There was corrupt justice that put Jesus to death — a kangaroo court, a juridical farce. The judges take bribes, said the prophets, and the poor people sit in jail. Corrupt justice means the story of Sacco and Vanzetti — flunky judges, false witnesses, concocted charges, political trials — on trial before a nation whipped into bigotry by the press.

There was another public power — the mob that fell in line with the ruling classes, chanting idiot slogans to heat up the blood in their veins. They want to see a crucifixion. They can be programmed to thrive on violence, to sink into sadism, and switch from the hosanna chants of one weekend to the cries, "Crucify him," on the very next. It is easy for us to get swept up into mob spirit and mob action, to get in line with the goose-stepping motions of a conservative crowd, the radical rabble, or the middle-class masses. Jesus experienced the invectives hurled from the mouths of intoxicated patriots.

There was still another power — the military. The soldiers were there to carry out the will of the ruling oligarchy. Jesus saw his nation drifting toward war, and his heart cried out for Jerusalem, "If only the people would have known the things that make for peace." But Jesus fell into the hands of the system that makes for wars. The soldiers did their usual thing. They had the weapons and so they used them. They stripped him and beat him and pressed the thorns into his scalp. They put a purple robe around him and saluted him. They blindfolded him and struck him and spit in his face. These were the professional soldiers who always fought in "just wars" as the "protective reaction" of Rome defending herself on foreign soil. All of Rome's wars were just wars. There is no other kind to those who wage the wars. They drove the spikes through his hands and feet. They gambled for his clothes. And Jesus was dead, literally dead.

That was the trip that Jesus took. He was wounded for our transgressions, he was bruised for our iniquities. Was it a beautiful trip? A bad trip? It was a real trip of Jesus into the public places exposed to worldly powers. He was not the victim of mere private and inner sins. He was caught in the web of a sinful world, linking all before him and since in a solidarity of evil systems, evil thoughts and deeds, to which we all contribute our share.

The powers that killed Jesus are the same powers that we support. He bore our sins. He felt them in his body and soul. In doing that he exposed them for what they are. Jesus took up the cross of public suffering. He did not flinch and turn away from the bitter cup. In some way, in a way we can only stutter to express, this was so total an act of self-surrender, so complete a response to the demands of freedom, so absolute a loving identification with the plight of all men trapped by those same deadly powers, that somehow it affected God. It became not only an act that can raise the consciousness of people concerning the powers that run their lives, but an act of God by which he takes up a new attitude toward mankind, holding out a new promise that these powers can be defeated. They will be defeated; they will not win in the end. They will not keep men enslaved forever. The cross of defeat and humiliation will not be the last word.

A new humanity will rise; a new potential will be created; a new set of options will come into view. The enemies of men and the enmity within them will exchange places with the crucified Jesus. They will be put to death; they will be buried in hell. He will rise to new life, and he will lead a new humanity into a new day.

By the story of Easter we learn that the victim of public violence becomes the victor for the sake of the violated. Because of that victory we are more than conquerors, going forth already now in a struggle with the powers in history, conquering in the spirit of Jesus and by the love that he revealed as the heart of God. We are no longer slaves but free men, free from religious bigotry, free from political graft and greed, from the corrupting of justice, the mob spirit, the military system, and free from the rule of these powers. And in this way we are also taking a Jesus trip. It is not so much a trip into ourselves, the nooks and crannies of our own inner life for its own sake, but the trip of those who enter into the struggle with the powers that rule this world. And in that way we participate in the death of Jesus, and share in the hope of the victory marked by his resurrection.

2

The

Powerlessness

of God

Luke 23:6-12: "When Pilate heard this, he asked whether the man was a Galilean. And when he learned that he belonged to Herod's jurisdiction, he sent him over to Herod, who was himself in Jerusalem at that time. When Herod saw Jesus, he was very glad, for he had long desired to see him, because he had heard about him, and he was hoping to see some sign done by him. So he questioned him at some length; but he made no answer. The chief priests and the scribes stood by, vehemently accusing him. And Herod with his soldiers treated him with contempt and mocked him; then, arraying him in gorgeous apparel, he sent him back to Pilate. And Herod and Pilate became friends with each other that very day, for before this they had been at enmity with each other."

King Herod appears in the Gospel story of Jesus as the representative of worldly power and tyrannical rule. Back in Bethlehem King Herod killed all the baby boys under two years old, but Jesus escaped with Mary and Joseph to Egypt. Later, when Jesus was becoming famous in Galilee, his cousin John was picked up by Herod's soldiers and put in jail. Herod was celebrating his birthday when he gave the command to have John's head cut off and carried in on a platter. King Herod represents arbitrary power seeking to become absolute. Jesus went on his way through towns and villages, preaching and teaching the kingdom of God. News of his fame reached Herod. One day some Pharisees came to Jesus and warned him, saying, "You'd better get out of here. Herod is looking for you, and wants to kill you." Now at last Herod had his big opportunity. The high priests handed Jesus over to Pilate, and Pilate handed him over to Herod. And Herod was glad to see him. He had heard about the many miracles and now he wanted to see him do a trick or two.

Webber and Rice capture some of the drama in the rock opera, *Jesus Christ Superstar*. Herod says:

> So you are the Christ, you're the great Jesus Christ
> Prove to me that you're divine — change my water into
>   wine . . . .
> So you are the Christ you're the great Jesus Christ
> Prove to me that you're no fool, walk across my
>   swimming pool . . . .
> Feed my household with this bread —
>   you can do it on your head.

But Jesus is silent. He answers not a word. And so Herod becomes irritated and exasperated:

> "Hey! Aren't you scared of me, Christ? Mr. Wonderful Christ!
> You're a joke, you're not the Lord —
>   you are nothing but a fraud
> Take him away — he's got nothing to say!
> Get out, you King of the Jews! Get out of my life!

The next time we hear about Herod, he is laying his filthy, violent hands on the early followers of Jesus. He killed James, the brother of John, with the sword, and when he saw how popular that was, he arrested Peter and put him in jail. Herod's power was going to his head. One day he put on his robes, took his seat upon the throne, and made a speech. The people shouted, "The voice of a god, and not of man!" Power corrupts, absolute power corrupts absolutely. That, according to Lord Acton, is the axiom of power.

Jesus is standing before naked power and he is powerless. Speechless, he offers no defense. He does nothing and says nothing. All the action is coming from the other side. The leading priests and their theologians are piling up the accusations; Herod and his soldiers are making fun of him. Jesus is a pawn in the power play of these very important people. Now, what should we do? Take up a collection and start a defense fund in behalf of this innocent man who is about to be mangled by the unmatched power of the state? Or should we do the very opposite, and assume that because Jesus has been accused and arraigned by the highest officials in the land, he is therefore guilty? Must we not assume there's some substance to the charges brought against him? After all, "where there's smoke, there's fire."

Jesus doesn't look around for any help. He doesn't expect his friends could even come to his defense. He's not crying out for justice or mercy. He's not making any speeches, insulting the inquisitor, or cracking any jokes. He's just there being pushed around like a helpless child. It was this sight of Jesus in total abject self-surrender, his boundless capacity to suffer mistreatment without whimpering, his refusal to resist the fiends of power with his own will-to-power; it was all this that Nietzsche found so unbelievably irritating and stupid. Nietzsche saw in Jesus' conduct an astounding "mixture of the sublime, the sick, and the childlike." It's completely laughable to apply such concepts as "hero" and "genius" to Jesus. Strictly speaking, Nietzsche said, "the only applicable word for Jesus' attitude before these worldly powers is 'idiot.' " After Nietzsche died his sister published his works; she found the term too shocking, so she deleted it. But Nietzsche meant it. It was his own peculiar way of saying that Jesus is a unique case. This is unlike anything you'll ever see in the world. It defies our usual categories of sanity, reason, and balance. So Nietzsche followed up this startling judgment with the statement, "Actually, there has been but one Christian, and he died on the cross." Nothing in Christianity and nothing in all of history is quite like this man

Jesus, in his encounter with the potentates of the world that indulge their will-to-power.

You and I know very well that, with all the Christian patience and courage we could muster on the spot, we could not suffer the way Jesus did. We could not hold our tongue the way he did. We could not bear up under the abuse of power the way Jesus did. We would cry, we would curse, we would fight, we would hate, we would rebel. Or maybe we would throw ourselves at the mercy of the court; maybe we would capitulate, maybe compromise, or join the system. Maybe we would become stool pigeons or turn state's evidence. Ah, maybe we could go free like Barabbas, maybe even live to rule someday ourselves. Then we would become a part of the reenactment of church history, of the powerful church, the church of the grand inquisitor, the church of the crusades, the church of worldly power, the church that sends its chaplains to war, to bless the violence of the nations. We would become part of the Judas-church that exists today. We would become members of the church of the Antichrist, because we would then take the name of Christ and place it on the side of Pilate and Herod and the chief priests.

In George Orwell's *1984* he has O'Brien saying, "If you want a picture of the future, imagine a boot stamping on a human face." All the powers of the world were then assembled to kill Jesus. But those very same powers have gone crazy in our time. If Herod massacred the children then, the slaughter of the innocents is going on in our day. If Herod took the head of John the Baptist who spoke out against the wickedness of those in high places, so today too the power system is out to cut the throats of those who speak against the vile works of wickedness in high places.

Our age has swallowed the dogma that the strong shall prevail over the weak, and may the best man win. Our age has become intoxicated with power, electric power, atomic power, military power, brute power. People are looking for their salvation in power terms. If students want to participate, they call for student power. If blacks seek freedom, they cry for black power. Saul Alinsky advised students and radicals to organize around middle-class power . . . "the new tinderbox of revolution."

The attractive thing about this power is that it brings results. Nkrumah of Ghana, the people's redeemer, once a student in a mission school, said, "Power politics is the way of salvation." So he paraphrased a Gospel saying this way, "Seek first the kingdom of politics and its power, and all these things will be yours."

That is the universal way of salvation in our age. The new nations are going the way of the old nations. The people seeking freedom are going the way of the slaveholders. The children of Israel are worshiping the Pharoah; Christians are not only paying taxes to Caesar, but are joining his army, and becoming the religious pimps for his kind of devastating and desacrating power.

Then there was Jesus in stark contrast. What was he doing with the powers? He said he could have had twelve legions of angels, but he let them capture him with swords and clubs, mock him, and spit on him. Nietzsche said there's no other word for it, but "idiot." St. Paul, however, saw more deeply into the matter. Standing in silent subjection and walking in surrendering submissiveness all the way to the cross, Jesus was making a public spectacle, Paul said, of those powers and was leading them as captives in his triumphal procession (Col. 2:15). The image comes from a Roman custom. When a Roman general defeated another country, he would march the rulers of that country into Rome on their bare feet, tagging behind the chariot on which he was riding in triumphant splendor. This was either an act of an idiot, or it was the power of God unto salvation, a new kind of power that can strip all the powers of their claim to divinity. This is the power to unmask the powers, to expose and defeat the powers in a game they cannot win. This is making a public spectacle of the powers. Jesus said, "I lay down my life . . . of my own accord. No one takes it from me" (John 10:17, 18).

A young lady who was a student leader on the Berkeley campus during the riots said, "We had to get arrested by the police. It was the only way to break the magic spell of fear they cast over all of us. Once in prison, we experienced a great freedom. Once on trial, we discovered the system of justice was only human like ourselves." That is demythologizing the powers, breaking their spell, their claim, their sphere of control, their absolute dominion.

Now many of us are crippled by a sense of powerlessness in this age of power monstrosities. We would like to see them cut down to size. But we don't know what to do. So we think, perhaps we'd better get hold of power ourselves and fight power with power. "All power to the people," the slogan goes. But do the people know how to handle power? Is power only a vice in the hands of aristocrats? Will the lust for power change into the power of love in the people's hands? Can the people turn water into wine and stones into bread? Are people, just plain people, the source of salvation?

Is that going to be the recipe of renewal for the church today? Some say, the trouble with the church is that it's losing its influence, it's losing its power, it's not where the action is, it doesn't speak out loud and clear and get others to listen. It had better get back into politics and come out of its religious seclusion, and get hold of some of that power to change the world. But a wise man said, "He who fights with monsters should be careful lest he thereby become a monster. And if thou gaze long into an abyss, the abyss will also gaze into thee" (Nietzsche).

The church has been too long one of the power monstrosities in the world. Is not that the sickness of the church that it has lived by power and now indulges in nostalgic homesickness for the power of yesteryear? It has not wanted to look the part of the idiot in the eyes of the power brokers of the world. The church has said to Caesar: "If you can do it, we can do it too." So they raised up a Pope with absolute power, with keys to enter the smoke-filled rooms of the secular power systems. Thus, the church has dealt with worldly power by matching it with her own ecclesiastical power. It is the power of Caiaphas and Annas and the chief priests, who stand by accusing Jesus of blasphemy and religious heresy.

The growing impotence of the church today is a new opportunity to believe in the gospel-power of Jesus which puts an end to the power of the world. Jesus is the eschatological event because of his absolute refusal to match power with power. If he would have walked across the swimming pool or come down from the cross, he would have extended the life of the powers. But he was putting the powers to death in his own dying. He was taking the divinity out of the powers, so they would lose their dominion and become servants to the praise of God and the liberation of mankind. The silence of Jesus is the powerlessness of love, the helplessness of God in the world that is ruled by the power monstrosities of the old age. The new age of soul power, of love power, of spirit power, is dawning in the powerlessness of Jesus before the powers-that-be.

Powerlessness is the new role of God in the rule of love. Bonhoeffer put it this way: "God allows himself to be edged out of the world and on to the cross. God is weak and powerless in the world, and that is exactly the way, the only way, in which he can be with us and help us." He says, "Only a suffering God can help." The utter obedience of Jesus, even unto death, without letting go of love and grabbing hold of power, meant a real identification of God with the suffering in this world, with those who are mocked, tortured, burned, and gassed, with those who are rendered powerless in the realms of power. Zechariah says, "This is the word of the Lord . . . : Not by might, nor by power, but by my Spirit, says the Lord of hosts" (Zech. 4:6).

Lent is a time to renounce the power and the thirst for power. It is a time to attack the sphere of the powers by vindicating the miracles of the Spirit in our lives. It is the Spirit of love-power. We are not that power, but we can bear witness to that power by joining those who become defenseless and utterly exposed to the principalities that rule the world and quench their thirst on the blood of the martyrs. A Christian is one who understands himself to be a joke if he does not take the side of the powerless in the power struggles in the world. If he does not, he is not even a little sign of the defeat of the powers in the powerlessness of Jesus and his love. Then he is only a member of Herod's military chorus or Caiaphas' glee club. To exist as a Christian in the world is to withhold all adoration of the powers, and to enter into the new power, the power of the man on the cross who was waging the war of God against the false gods of power with the weapon of love. Because of this love, and its dying to power, we can have new possibilities of life beyond the death-dealing blows of the power-monsters in this world. He died for us that we might live to love, that we might love to live.

3

The
Trial of
Truth

Matt. 26:57 ff.: "Then those who had seized Jesus led him to Caiaphas the high priest, where the scribes and the elders had gathered. But Peter followed him at a distance, as far as the courtyard of the high priest, and going inside he sat with the guards to see the end. Now the chief priests and the whole council sought false testimony against Jesus that they might put him to death, but they found none, though many false witnesses came forward. At last two came forward and said, 'This fellow said, "I am able to destroy the temple of God, and to build it in three days." ' And the high priest stood up and said, 'Have you no answer to make? What is it that these men testify against you?' But Jesus was silent. And the high priest said to him, 'I adjure you by the living God, tell us if you are the Christ, the Son of God.' Jesus said to him, 'You have said so. But I tell you, hereafter you will see the Son of man seated at the right hand of Power, and coming on the clouds of heaven.' Then the high priest tore his robes, and said, 'He has uttered blasphemy. Why do we still need witnesses? You have now heard his blasphemy. What is your judgment?' They answered, 'He deserves death.' "

Jesus our Lord was placed on trial. We have read only a small part of the court proceedings, but you have read the whole thing many times. It was not the trial of a single man who had been hopelessly misunderstood. This was the trial of truth. It was the system rejecting the truth that came to deliver us from evil, from the evil of ignorance, from the evil of injustice, from the evil of callous hearts and self-serving appetites. Jesus could not walk through our world without a call going out for his arrest, without being grabbed by the police, jeered by the crowd, brought to trial, first before the highest authorities of religion, then the highest authority of government. Jesus did not last long in this world. He kept his mouth shut for thirty years, but when he began to open up and declare his meaning, the wheels of the social machinery were set in motion against him. He bore the truth within him; he was the minister of truth, the man of truth. He said it himself before Pilate, "Everyone who is of the truth hears my voice," and Pilate said, "What is truth?"

Truth has to struggle for any headway in our world. It comes up against fraudulent court proceedings, kangaroo courts, mock trials, the framing and condemning of innocent men, false swearing, stacked juries, dirty jails, and finally, the gallows, the cross, the gas chamber, or possibly years on death row while an appeal is being made. Our world does not distinguish between the man of truth and evil men. The man of truth is subjected to the same treatment. The more purely a man tells the truth, the easier it is to mistake him for an evil man. Thus Jesus could not escape mingling with sinners and being mangled by a system that was not prepared to distinguish between qualitatively different kinds of threats to itself. Rampant and unchecked evil is a threat to any order of life. The established system has to protect itself through laws and courts and the police. But truth is also a threat, and the system gives it the same treatment. So Jesus died between two criminals. And no one could tell the difference. He was counted as less worthy of being released than Barabbas, a notorious prisoner. Truth had to go the way of the criminal; it had to suffer the criminal's fate and die a criminal's death. Truth is a crime against the establishment — whether the establishment of religion, with its high priests and elders, or the establishment of the state, with its governors and judges.

We cannot forget some other memorable trials of truth. One happened four hundred years before Christ, another fifteen hundred years after him — the trial of Socrates and the trial of Martin Luther. The most precious truth handed down to us from the past is usually resurrected from the death-dealing blows of a public trial. Truth that has not been placed on trial is not worth having; untried truth is only the conventional thing — the religious, moral, or social conventions of an established way of life. Once I had a chance to stand before the prison cell of Socrates. He ended his life in a clash with the religious and political authorities of the city of Athens. The system of justice could not tolerate the presence of this gadfly for truth.

Look at the charges: "Socrates, you are disloyal to the state, you are corrupting the minds of the young, irreligious, a complete atheist, because the things we call gods you say are no gods, like the sun and the moon." So Socrates was told that if he'd tone down and compromise the truth, mix some of the truth of God with the lies of the system, he could survive till a ripe old age. But Socrates replied with this speech:

> Men of Athens, I honor and love you, but I shall obey God rather than you, and while I have life and strength I shall never cease from the practice and teaching of philosophy, exhorting anyone whom I meet . . . . I believe that no greater good has ever happened in the state than my service to God. I would have you know that if you kill a person like me, you will be injuring yourselves more than you can injure me.

But they all condemned Socrates as deserving death.

Truth that is caught in the machinery of law and justice suffers the fate of the common criminal. That is the story of Lent. It happened again with Martin Luther. The machinery went into high gear to get rid of the truth he preached. Luther was called before the highest authority, the emperor. Certainly he was scared. He wrote to his friend Staupitz at this time, that great non-polarizer of the sixteenth century: "This is no time to cringe, but to cry aloud when our

Lord Jesus Christ is damned, reviled, and blasphemed."
Luther knew that a man who takes upon himself the burden
of truth has been united to the truth of Christ, and he cannot
be too proud to accept the same fate for himself. When we
see truth suffer, we see Christ suffer; when truth is mocked,
Christ is mocked. It was this identification which stood up
with Luther on trial before the emperor. "He who confesses
me before men, him will I confess in the presence of my
father, and he who denies me before men, him will I deny."
But the powers-that-be did not care a fig about the truth that
Luther preached. What they pounced on was that he was a
revolutionary. They charged him with inciting the German
people to riot. It was said, "Luther claims that the Germans
should wash their hands in the blood of the papists." Luther
was a detestable Bohemian heretic; he would have to be
imprisoned, and all his books burned. He was a devil in the
habit of a monk. In the Edict of Worms it was charged that
his teachings were fostering rebellion, polarization, war,
murder, robbery, arson, and would bring about the collapse
of Christendom. Luther lived the life of a beast, it said. He
was to be regarded as a convicted heretic, and no one was to
put him up. All his books were to be burned, and his teachings blotted from the memory of mankind.

It shows that you can put truth on trial, but you cannot
burn it. You cannot blot it out. The system can put its heavy
hand on the man of truth, and even nail him to a tree, but
the resurrection of truth goes on. Jesus said, "I am the way,
the truth, and the life." "I am the resurrection and the life."
I may have to die at the hands of high priests and the makers
of the law, and those who sit high up in the seats of justice. I
may have to alienate the crowd and take upon my head a
crown of thorns, but my truth shall rise again, and truth shall
win out. It will be broadcast over the whole earth, and every
tongue shall confess and every knee shall bow before the
Lord of truth.

Meanwhile the trial of truth goes on; the passion of Christ
is being reenacted in our world today. We have only this

promise to hand on — those who suffer for truth's sake suffer with Christ, and Christ with them.

Now, an ethical postscript about what this might mean for us today. If the trial of truth goes on today, and if Christ who is the truth is the subject of every such trial, what does this mean?

(1) It means that we have to participate in the trial of truth. (2) It means that we can never simply presume in favor of the prevailing system of law and justice. (3) It means that we cannot wash our hands as Pilate did, as though we are not fully guilty when "they" carry the truth away to be nailed to the cross. We are guilty. (4) It means that when truth is on trial, we cannot stand by outside the proceedings, warming ourselves by a cozy fire like Peter did when he denied Jesus. (5) It means that we must be in solidarity with those on trial, knowing that the messenger of the ultimate truth of God was accused of crimes against the state and the high priests of the established system. (6) It means, too, that we might have to go down without making any heroic speeches of the caliber of Socrates' and Luther's, that we might have to be more like the man of sorrows who was silent, when he had not a word to say.

Truth might have to suffer in silence; in weakness and humility it might find its power in the eloquence of silence. It may be just this power of silence that can bring to light the infinite and eternal meaning of Jesus' passion and death, the unique and incomparable reality of his suffering for all men. A word on his own behalf would have limited his truth, so that it is precisely in his defenselessness that he could become the defense of all the weak, and those who have no words to speak on their own behalf. The gospel is the story of the infinite suffering of the truth of God in Jesus of Nazareth, for us men and for our salvation, in a world that has not yet found a way to make room for truth and love.

4

Our Elected

Representative

A statement by Reinhold Niebuhr has stuck in my mind: the most simple confession of Christian faith, one that underlies all the very complicated doctrines of atonement, is that "Christ died for our sins." Let me read a few of the familiar verses from the New Testament that Niebuhr must have had in mind.

Rom. 5:8 "But God shows his love *for us* in that while we were yet sinners Christ *died for us*."

Rom. 8:32: "He who did not spare his own Son but gave him up *for us* all, will he not also give us all things with him?"

Gal. 3:13: "Christ redeemed us from the curse of the law, having become a curse *for us*—for it is written, 'Cursed be every one who hangs on a tree.'"

Eph. 5:2: "And walk in love, as Christ loved us and gave himself up *for us*, a fragrant offering and sacrifice to God."

1 Thess. 5:10: "[Our Lord Jesus Christ] *died for us* so that whether we wake or sleep we might live with him."

1 John 3:16: "By this we know love, that he laid down his life *for us*; and we ought to lay down our lives for the brethren."

Titus 2:14: "[Jesus Christ, our great God and Savior] gave himself *for us* to redeem us from all iniquity and to purify for himself a people of his own who are zealous for good deeds."

In these verses Christ is pictured as doing something for us, surrendering himself, sacrificing himself, giving himself up, in short, dying for us. We know that Christ died, that he died on the cross, and we believe that in some way he did this for us. But how and why? What role is Christ playing for us? It has been said that this means that Christ is our substitute. He is a scapegoat or whipping boy. This is the leading idea in one of the doctrines of the atonement. But how is Christ really our substitute? The word *substitute* does not appear in the New Testament. It comes as a later interpretation, to get at the meaning of confessing that "Christ died for us." But is Christ willing really to be our substitute? Does one who loves another want to take our place? To displace us? In ordinary life we must watch out for people who want to stand in as our substitutes. On every ball team, there are the first-string players, then the substitutes. When a substitute is sent in, he is competing for the place of the first stringer. The sub goes in and tries his hardest to become the permanent replacement. It happened a few years ago with the Baltimore Colts at the quarterback position. Johnny Unitas was the indispensable man, the key to the fabulous success of the Colts. Then he injured his arm. His substitute, Earl Morrall, went in and won fifteen ball games in a row, taking over Johnny Unitas's job as the permanent first-string quarterback.

Our society is like an athletic team. It is competitive; the better your job, the more eager people are to take your place. The substitute does not go in to represent you, to keep your place open until you return. Not at all. The substitute goes in to shine, to replace you, to explode the myth of the indispensable man. When LBJ was politically wounded and bleeding, there were many eager to take his place. A competitive society forgets its indispensable men very quickly. No wonder we do not like the role of the substitute in our society. We do not want to be supplanted, shoved aside; we do not want someone to take our place, to dislodge us, to overshadow our identity. Moreover, it is not true that Jesus is our substitute; for we still have our grief; we still have our pain;

we still have to die. Christ suffered for us; but he did not suffer instead of us. We still have to suffer. Christ died for us, but he did not die instead of us; we still have to die.

But if he is not our substitute in the sense that he replaces us, he can be our representative. That is what we need in our competitive society. Who can represent me in a world in which I am replaceable, in a society in which I am worth only what I can produce, when there is always someone who can produce just as well and as much as I can? Who can represent me without replacing me? Who will keep a place open for me, when I am sick or away on leave? Who will represent me as my defense attorney when my case is hopeless? Who will represent me when my voice is silenced by death? Who will tell me that I am a unique, indispensable, irreplaceable individual, that I count ultimately, even in a society in which every role can be played just as well by someone else, in which for every job there are many qualified applicants, for every person a machine ready to take over?

There is little wonder that the problem of personal identity has become an open festering sore in the sick body of our social life. What have the students been revolting for? Behind the big words about war and peace, justice and the international order, about participatory democracy and a new university, there is the crying out for personal identity. Who am I? How am I to become authentic, a true individual self in a world supermarket, in which everything has its price tag, and a person is equal only to the sum of his functions, and these functions in turn can be taken over by someone else or even better by a machine? It is in this world of carbon copies, of mass-produced salable goods, that the individual cries out for representation, for representation without displacement.

Christ is able to give us such representation. He is our representative; but he is not a substitute who wants to step in to replace us. Jesus' death on the cross has representative meaning. His whole life was representative. He represented the interests of others ultimately; he did not use people in his own selfish interest. He did not go about worrying over his good name and reputation; he wept but never for himself; he suffered, but not on his own account. He went ahead, not to get there first, but to prepare a place for all of us. Jesus can deal with a man's identity crisis, because he was not hung up on his own. Jesus' entire life was representing the good things of God's kingdom — healing power for the sick, hope for the dying, forgiveness for sinners, amnesty for outcasts, and a voice for the poor.

Faith is an act of letting Jesus be our representative, for in representing us, he never replaces us. Because he died for us, we never die alone without representation, without hope for personal identity even beyond death. We never have to die alone on a godforsaken hill outside the gate. We can die in a communion of his love, in the assurance of the forgiveness of sins, with undying hope for life and resurrection. Because Jesus died the death of the sinner as the sinless man, Jesus can be our representative. Because he died the death of the guilty one, as the guileless man, he can be our representative. Because he died the death under the law as the man of love, full of life to share and taking time for others, he can be our representative. He can be our representative because, in being raised from the dead, he was approved by God as having the right credentials to be the ambassador of the human race.

But Jesus is more than our representative; he is God's representative. He is not a substitute for God. It is the essence of heathenism to make substitutes for God. Jesus stands in for God as the one who represents God's love for us. In Jesus' suffering God himself is taking part in the pain of each one of us. To believe in the cross of Jesus is to let God suffer for us. Bonhoeffer's words make the point: Only a suffering God can help! In the ancient church the question was raised, can the Father suffer? Can he experience pain? And the church fathers said, "No." But now we would raise some doubts about that. It would be a strange Father who would not let himself in for any of the pain his Son is suffering. To believe in a God who does not suffer great pain in a world of pain is too much to ask.

We have used the word *representative* to speak of Jesus' role in dying for us. That word does not appear in the New Testament either. It is an interpretation of the words *for us.* Jesus is there for us, representing us without replacing us. Jesus is there for God, representing God without replacing him. By being absolutely open to men, Jesus was able to open them up to God. By being absolutely open to God, Jesus was able to open up God's heart to men. By identifying God to us, Jesus is able to answer our quest for identity. There is no answer to the identity crisis, the question "Who am I?" by looking to this or that thing, to this or that job, to this or that hope, to this or that future. Jesus is the representative in whom God and man can exchange hope for each other.

Many times we feel like giving up, giving up on ourselves, giving up on God. And then we hear the good word, that Jesus gave himself up *for us.* For Jesus' sake God does not give up on us. Jesus helps God define himself to us, at a time when we have a lot of questions about who God is and what he is up to.

It used to be thought that it was only man who needed to have a representative to plead his case before God. It used to be thought that without Christ God would get rid of us, or forget about us. That is surely true, but the other side appears now to be equally true. God needs to have a representative to plead *his* case before man. Now it appears that God is on trial, that man is ready to get rid of a God who does not seem to be doing much these days to change the world for the better. The revolution is on, but is God with it? For this reason God needs one like Jesus to make his own case credible in a world of pain and death, of death camps and rockets and napalm. It is Christ who gives us reason to hope that God is alive and still involved in the human adventure. It is Christ who makes the connection between God's presence in the world and human suffering, so that we can believe that reconciliation can come from death, that victory can be forged from tragedy, that fulfillment of life can arise in spite of defeat, that resurrection can convert a cross into the good news of God in our suffering, in our pain, in our dying. So whether we live or whether we die, we have a representative through whom God identifies with us, and in whom we have a promise of identity that goes infinitely beyond any word our world can speak to us or that we can speak to ourselves.

5

Jesus,

Our Revolutionary

Leader

Matt. 22:34-46: "But when the Pharisees heard that he had silenced the Sadducees, they came together. And one of them, a lawyer, asked him a question, to test him. 'Teacher, which is the great commandment in the law?' And he said to him, 'You shall love the Lord your God with all your heart, and with all your soul, and with all your mind. This is the great and first commandment. And a second is like it, You shall love your neighbor as yourself. On these two commandments depend all the law and the prophets.'

"Now while the Pharisees were gathered together, Jesus asked them a question, saying, 'What do you think of the Christ? Whose son is he?' They said to him, 'The son of David.' He said to them, 'How is it then that David, inspired by the Spirit, calls him Lord, saying,

' "The Lord said to my Lord,
    Sit at my right hand,
        till I put thy enemies under thy feet"?
If David thus calls him Lord, how is he his son?' And no one was able to answer him a word, nor from that day did any one dare to ask him any more questions."

The atmosphere is again charged with electrifying talk about revolution. Students are no longer satisfied to be oriented in the usual way. University freshmen received a brochure called "Disorientation," warning them to distrust most of what the university says and does. Seminarians took part in a "counterorientation" at People's Church. They heard the call for revolution by speaker after speaker. Many have the conviction that we are going to be in for another hot year, that a lot of heat and anger have still to be released into America because nothing has really changed. Killing and crime continue at home and abroad; the blacks won't let us forget that poverty, hunger, and injustice have not dwindled by one degree; and students are still calling for an alternative to an educational system that is content to make spare parts for the social and political machine into which they would like to throw a monkey wrench.

With the whirl of these pressures and collisions around us, it would be surprising if we as Christians would not look to the story of Jesus to see whether we have a word, or a model, or a promise, or a sign, or something that can help us, direct us, to clue us in as to where to stand, when to march, how to act.

If only we could begin to see in a new way the revolutionary dimensions of Jesus' ministry, well for one thing, it might prevent us from joining the wrong revolutions. There are going to be a lot of revolutions still that will be bad news for human beings, for ordinary people, especially for those at the bottom. But there is a revolution of which Jesus is the leader. He read his manifesto first in the Synagogue, reading from the prophet Isaiah:

> The Spirit of the Lord is upon me,
> because he has appointed me to preach good news to the poor,
> He has sent me to proclaim release to the captives
> And recovering of sight to the blind,
> To set at liberty those who are oppressed.

This is a one-sided platform of ministry; it would guarantee defeat in a national election. It is taking sides in the struggle of life for the poor, for people locked up in jails, for the blind, that is, for people deprived of medical care and a liberating education, in short, for all those oppressed in any way. What is revolutionary about Jesus' ministry is that he never talked about gradual measures, minor improvements, piecemeal changes, or just a little bit of progress. He had an all-or-nothing way of speaking. He was not for reform, but for repentance; he was not for arbitration but for conversion. He did not talk about the happy medium, the middle way, or peace negotiations. It is the mark of his revolutionary style to speak in absolutes, in total terms, complete transvaluation, involving a reversal of signs so that plus is minus and minus is plus.

I would like to try to portray Jesus as a unique revolutionary figure in thought and action. It will present us a dilemma I cannot resolve. The church has tried for two thousand years, but it has never succeeded in solving the riddle of Jesus' own revolutionary personality. The best minds in theology still spend the prime of their life in trying to figure out what Jesus was up to in the world.

Jesus began his revolution with the message: "Repent, for the kingdom of God is at hand." The revolutionary morality of that message comes out in the Great Commandment: Love God in an absolute way, and love your neighbor as yourself. But this morality is based on the deeper revolutionary initiative of God himself. When Jesus represents the kingdom of God, he brings the love of God first of all, again in a one-sided way, to those in terrible need of repentance. They are sinners, unpatriotic and subversive people, prostitutes and morally impure people. He brings forgiveness to them. He does not debate with these people about the law or their sin. They know they are in trouble and need to be loved and accepted. In spite of the fact that society rejects them, the One who judges society itself accepts them. This frees them from having to base their dignity and pride in themselves on social acceptability. That is the dynamite which sets off the demand for society to be changed, to give expression to the new freedom, that wide range of freedom which God has brought into the experience of forgiven sinners. To call simply for external changes in society without touching the nerves of freedom in the internal experience and consciousness of men, grounded in God's loving acceptance of the sinner, is not a very great revolution.

The kingdom comes and is brought near to the poor and the oppressed people first, because they are the only ones ready for a great reversal in the order of things. Even to be told to repent is good news, because it holds out some hope for change, some chance to be swept up by the transforming power of God. The call of the kingdom is not to become a little better, but for a radical turning away from the old life you've been living to a new life. In this new life there are deeds to be done. There is a demand for revolutionary consistency. Some only hear the word, they go to church a lot. Some only speak the word; if they are pretty good at that, they might become preachers or professors. And then there are those who *do it.* They are the blessed ones who enter the kingdom; they are creatively involved in the world liberation movement, helping to raise people from the graveyards of degradation, stinking decay and destruction.

Jesus preached a hard revolutionary line. When the kingdom of God, the rule of his love, claims a person, Jesus said, one must sacrifice all personal property. One must leave parents, home, and country. Extreme measures are called for — an offending eye must be plucked out and an evil-doing hand cut off. One must be prepared to be despised, harassed and ostracized by society. A clean choice has got to be made. God and Mammon cannot both be served; either you carry the cross of the kingdom or you seek the security of the establishment. "Whoever does not renounce all that he has cannot be my disciple." This unconditional surrender of all your heart and soul and mind to the rule of God's love means this: if you give your whole life away like that, well, that is the only way to find it.

We have come to the third step in the revolutionary scheme of Jesus. The first was that, when God arrives with his kingdom, he does not come in at the top; he enters society from the bottom, holding out his love and forgiveness and creative power to those left out. The second step was that this invitation calls for an about-face — not conformity to society, but conversion to the kingdom. Now the third step is where the bomb goes off, where the pillars of society have to crack and crumble. For the dramatic reversal of the relationship between God and man, such that the poor and the hungry and the oppressed are the point of contact for the inrushing power of God's rule, signals new thrusts and new directions and opens up a new vision of a more human society, calling for a dramatic reversal in the relations between men. That gets down to the nitty-gritty of social morality, economic systems, and political structures. For when the kingdom touches a human being, it is not calling for his integration into society the way it is; it calls him to change society.

The power of God's love does not merely give you courage to endure your lot, to put up with things the way they are. Then God's love would be a hollow consolation. The love of God is translated as love for the neighbor. That love forbids the person who hears the word of liberation and release to reintegrate himself into the social system which crushed him and oppressed him in the first place. He must go back into the system as the forgiven sinner now with new love for his neighbor, with a mission to attack the sources of degradation, decay, and humiliation, and to create a new basis for human dignity and freedom and happiness.

This revolutionary dream of moving our human and social life into the zone of freedom and liberation and wholeness and happiness can be dismissed as a mere dream. A lot of Christians have handled Jesus and his message that way. It's a noble dream, but it's only a dream. It's a great utopia, but it's not for this world; it's a nice hope, but Jesus was only using figures of speech to talk about another world, some other world than this one.

Well, we can't do that, for when Jesus preached repentance, and announced the coming of God's kingdom, and brought good news to the poor and hope to the outcasts, he never hedged his message with reservations about time and place. This is what makes him a revolutionary. His demands are not whittled down to adjust to our everyday life. He presses the demands, and in doing so he does not hint that He's only exaggerating for effect. It is like playing poker according to the rules of chess. That's not easy. So as a revolutionary Jesus is saying, when the kingdom comes, you're in a brand new kind of game. Do you want to train for it? Are you ready to dedicate yourself to its rule — the rule of God's love? Jesus does not make it look easy; he does not speak as though he expects a crowd to follow him. He never dreamed of founding a church which thinks in terms of big numbers and big buildings and big budgets, of being the majority, of filling huge cathedrals with mobs of middle-class people sitting on their pride of having made it cozy and comfortable for themselves, content to leave the others out.

Jesus spoke in negatives as though to warn us against trying to enter the kingdom. He was a poor salesman; he told how rough things would be. He spoke of the kingdom as though he really didn't expect anyone would have the guts to try it. Perhaps he was expecting at most a tiny cadre of followers, of faithful disciples. So he said, "My little band of revolutionaries has got to be different." You must not get angry or swear; you must not be a hypocrite; you must not see the splinter in your brother's eye, and don't brag about your good deeds; don't put lots of money in the bank; that's no real security in the inflationary times of human existence. And don't worry about tomorrow; it takes the joy and humor out of today. Don't be greedy and full of spite. If you lose, don't get mad at the guy who beat you. Say, nice going, good shot, not out of pretense and good manners, but from the heart. When you pray, don't show off, using nice religious words and the meaningless repetition of ritualistic phrases.

That would be enough to make a person resign right now from the revolution headed up by Jesus. But he goes on — and on — and on, to make the revolutionary rhetoric and slogans and schemes and programs you hear today quite pallid, boring, cheap, and easy by comparison. Don't just love your friends and neighbors; love your enemy. It's easy to pray for your loved ones. Try praying for those who persecute you. Don't seek revenge, but get the hate out of your heart. If someone enjoys hitting you on the cheek, give him the other one also. Give and expect nothing in return. If someone swipes the shirt off your back, give him your coat; he might need that too.

I've gone to church many years, and heard lots of sermons. About this time, it has usually been the role of the clever preacher to soften these hard sayings of Jesus. He has gone to school to learn some tricks of interpretation, to make it sound that these words of Jesus are really quite compatible with our everyday existence and the basic structures of the society we happen to be in. The revolutionary sting is pulled; the words are blurred; we take them in as just part of the healthy diet of everyman in the world. Maybe we let Jesus pass as a liberal reformer. But he really wasn't that. He was an eschatological revolutionary, and if we don't care or can't stand to live from his words in this imperfect world, we have no right to defer them to another world, to spiritualize away their revolutionizing power.

The alternative is to let Jesus come at us again and again as the enigmatic person whose revolution is unique, which does not fit into any ready-made world. This revolutionary word and model can be the ever-living source of a revolutionizing process in which we are continually engaged. We can be in the struggle to realize and materialize the good news to the poor and liberation to the oppressed. All men are equal, children of one Father; therefore, social differences of class and position must fall away. But they won't fall away of themselves. They must be attacked. A life-style founded on love and care for others must assault the distinction between insiders and outsiders, friends and enemies, relatives and strangers. For the first shall be last; sinners enter the kingdom first; the greatest person is the servant of others; the exalted ones are an abomination to God. The rich man must sell all he has, to share with the poor. This is why it is so hard for the rich to enter the kingdom. When you throw a party, invite the poor, the lame and the maimed, and those who can't pay you back. That is a revolution; the kingdom of God as mediated through Jesus is the revolution. It means the hungry must be fed, strangers welcomed, the naked clothed, the sick healed, and children loved and educated — all of them.

With Jesus as our revolutionary leader, and with this hard-line revolutionizing program, involving tough doctrine and radical action, we would make a mistake to trade our Christian revolution in on some other fake imitation of the real thing.

A theological student hit the nail on the head, when he said, we must transform the saying of Che Guevara: "The vocation of every lover is to bring about revolution" into "The duty of every revolution is to bring about love." The Great Commandment is still today what the revolution of God in the world is all about. Jesus is our revolutionary hero, in whom that revolution of love is fully incarnate, so that we confess, Jesus is our God, Lord, and Savior.

6

Ascension:

The Homecoming

of the

Son

Acts 1:6-11: "So when they had come together, they asked him, 'Lord, will you at this time restore the kingdom to Israel?' He said to them, 'It is not for you to know times or seasons which the Father has fixed by his own authority. But you shall receive power when the Holy Spirit has come upon you; and you shall be my witnesses in Jerusalem and in all Judea and Samaria and to the end of the earth.' And when he had said this, as they were looking on, he was lifted up, and a cloud took him out of their sight. And while they were gazing into heaven as he went, behold, two men stood by them in white robes, and said, 'Men of Galilee, why do you stand looking into heaven? This Jesus, who was taken up from you into heaven, will come in the same way as you saw him go into heaven.' "

When we celebrate the ascension of Christ, it is hard to do so if we do not know exactly what we are celebrating. The stories tell us that Jesus went away. But where did he go? He disappeared behind a cloud and went up into heaven. When that happened the disciples went back to Jerusalem, jumping with joy! That is extremely odd behavior. Think of all the odd pictures in Christian art. You can see the disciples huddling together on top of a hill. They are looking upward, with fear and surprise on their faces. Above the hill the figure of Jesus is floating upward through a cloud. In some paintings you can only see the feet which have not yet been enveloped by the cloud. That is what comes to mind when we think of the ascension. If ever one would feel justified in demythologizing, this would be the time to do it with a vengeance.

The story tells us that Jesus went away. So we are bound to ask, where did he go? If we try to answer that literally in a spatial picture, if he literally went up into space like a rocket, our minds are filled with foolish and stupid thoughts — like the fundamentalist press which answered the news headline that the Russians had put a man in space with the claim that Jesus had beat them to it. Jesus was the first man in space.

But the process of demythologizing the ascension of Christ as the movement from one place to another in space is not something that began with the name of Rudolf Bultmann. Many church fathers, and Luther too, ridiculed that as a childish idea. Jesus did not float off into space like a balloon! But what happened then, and what are we to celebrate on the day of ascension?

I think we are to celebrate two things at least. The story of the ascension meets us as the culmination of the resurrection appearances of Jesus and his entrance into the hiddenness of God. If we ask: where did Jesus go? we must say he went to the Father. If you know where the Father is, that is where Jesus is. As Karl Barth puts it, the ascension is the story of the homecoming of the Son of Man who had wandered into a far country, a homecoming to the Father's house. The ascension story is a saga of the exaltation of Jesus to complete unity with the Father.

In the ancient world, in the world into which the message of Christ entered, there was an old saga of the ascension of Romulus into heaven. It was also the case that there were ascension stories about philosophers, for example, Appollonius of Tyana. In the Old Testament there was the ascension of Elijah and also of Enoch. It is clear that the story of ascension is one of exaltation, of being lifted up on high, so we say in our creed, he sits on the right hand of the Father, at the position of power, rulership, and honor. Jesus had gone to the Father, and because that is so, we who follow Jesus know where we are going.

Secondly, it was the beginning of something new in history. This is why the disciples went back to Jerusalem full of joy, praising and blessing God. John 16:7 tells us that Jesus looked upon his going away to the Father as the beginning of something new and much greater. "It is to your advantage that I go away." The absence of Christ means a new form of his presence.

The ascension at first seems like the reversal of the incarnation, so that the Son only retreats to where he came from. For this reason a thinker like Thomas Alitzer simply rejects it out of hand. But actually the ascension was an advance, not a retreat to the previous position of the Son with the Father. It was an advance to be signaled by the coming of the Spirit.

As Christians we believe paradoxically that Jesus went away so that he could be really present, so that he could be present in Chicago, in Africa, in India, in Vietnam, so that he could be present on both sides of every curtain that we erect, so that he could be present on both sides of the generation gap, so that he can be present this morning in the things we do and say in remembrance of him. Blessed are those who have not seen and yet believe.

Thus, ascension takes place between Easter and Pentecost. It is nothing by itself, but an occasion to celebrate that in Easter God has raised Jesus, preparing the way for the homecoming of the Son of Man, and an occasion to look ahead to Pentecost, the day of the outpouring of the Spirit, when many new gifts would rain down upon men, and a new history would be opened up, the history of the church in the world, to prepare all men and nations for their final homecoming in the house of the One Father of all.

7

Preparation for
Christmas

Phil. 2:5-11: "Have this mind among yourselves, which you have in Christ Jesus, who, though he was in the form of God, did not count equality with God a thing to be grasped, but emptied himself, taking the form of a servant, being born in the likeness of men. And being found in human form he humbled himself and became obedient unto death, even death on a cross. Therefore God has highly exalted him and bestowed on him the name which is above every name, that at the name of Jesus every knee should bow, in heaven and on earth and under the earth, and every tongue confess that Jesus Christ is Lord, to the glory of God the Father."

John 1:14: "And the Word became flesh and dwelt among us, full of grace and truth; we have beheld his glory, glory as of the only Son from the Father."

The feeling of joy is a constant refrain in the Christmas stories of the New Testament. When Mary announced to Elizabeth that she was to be a vessel of messianic fulfillment, even the babe in Elizabeth's womb leaped for joy. When the wise men from the East saw the star, they rejoiced exceedingly. When the angel appeared to the shepherds, he said, "Be not afraid; for behold, I bring you good news of a great joy which will come to all the people."

The Christmas hymns of our tradition resound with the same joyful theme: "A great and mighty wonder, this joyful feastday brings"; "Christians awake, Salute the happy morn"; "All my heart this night rejoices"; "The happy Christmas comes once more"; "Good Christian men, rejoice, With heart and soul and voice"; "I am so glad each Christmas eve, The night of Jesus' birth." And there are dozens more.

Yet for many modern men this spontaneous joy has been dampened, if not with sadness, at least with doubts and bewilderment. It is not easy for us to punctuate these Christmas stories with exclamation marks of joy. Rather, we tend to punctuate them with question marks or we raise all kinds of questions which they are too innocent to answer. The miracle of Christmas is accompanied by angels speaking, but we have seen no angels, by a moving star, but stars do not move in modern astronomy, by royal astrologers, but astrology today is a science of crackpots, a celestial choir of angels, but can this be more than poetry? Then there is the story of the birth from a virgin, which many Christians doubt or consider irrelevant to their faith.

Besides such details, there is the story as a whole which many in our audiences recognize as a fabulous mythology. True, in the space age and the race to the moon, modern man has gained the capacity to believe almost anything, even such fables as creatures from outer space — UFO's landing on earth in flying saucers. Christians would be foolhardy, however, to make this an analogy for believing in the incarnation of the Son of God in space and time, in human flesh.

Theological debate in the last twenty years has been in turmoil over the question of myth in the New Testament. The whole pattern of conceiving of a preexistent heavenly being coming down from beyond the skies to walk around on earth for some years, wearing the garments of human existence, and then returning beyond the clouds into heaven again, has been classified as mythological. The debate over this begins to dampen our joy, to throw us into the key of argument, rather than into the mood of joy, praise, and thanksgiving.

All of us are modern men. No serious Christian can escape the questions and doubts which our culture forces upon us, and within which we must bear a message of glad tidings. As

Christians we have to think seriously about how we are to present the miracle of Christmas to ourselves and to listeners who are culturally conditioned to doubt. There is one kind of preaching which certainly does not help, and that is to bludgeon, to scold, to threaten modern men because of their doubts. That only makes matters worse. It breeds guilt, more doubt, suspicion, and more hostility against the Christmas message. Nor will it do to ask man to sacrifice his intellect, and to believe unbelievable stories. Psychologically, this results not in salvation, but in destruction, and leads to schizophrenia — where your conscious will-power drives you to believe something that just will not go down. A Christian must at least be honest. We cannot hear the Christmas message with joy by going around serious questions which our age is asking; we must take these questions, and go through them, and beyond them. We must be more honest than those who ask the questions.

If we will be honest, we need not be helpless. The Gospel of Christmas is too great a miracle to be dissolved by the acids of modern doubt. If the miracle of Christmas is truly of God, and is a salvation event for all men, it will renew and justify the traditions of memory, and create new ones. So we start off with a simple trust that we can grasp in our faith and understanding as well as men of any previous age. Let us not paint ourselves into the corner where we presume that modern man has outgrown the gospel or can believe the gospel only by becoming credulous, naive, and primitive in his outlook. A man must believe the gospel while standing fully in his culture, not by jumping out of it into some more primitive culture, when it was presumably easier to believe in such things as angels, incarnations, celestial voices, and miracles of all kinds.

I believe that we can joyfully and honestly proclaim the mystery of the incarnation of the Son of God, and in such a way that faith in the Incarnate Lord becomes a genuine possibility for any modern man. Whether we will do this is another matter. If the appearance of Jesus Christ in the history of humanity is proclaimed at all in the manner in which we tell the stories of Santa Claus coming to town, then of course it will make no sense. Then we have no reason to decry the substitute of Santa Claus for Jesus Christ in the modern celebrations of the Christmas season. I suppose that this year, like in every previous year, many pulpits will be ranting and raving against the secularization of Christmas. The slogan, "Let's put Christ back into Christmas," will be the main course on the menu of preaching. At that rate our congregations will only hear some good or bad advice, but no gospel. Then they will witness the self-righteous piety of the preacher, rather than see the glimmerings of the glory of God in the gospel of Christ who brings joy and gladness.

1. INCARNATION AND RESURRECTION

The first observation is that we must not blow up Christmas out of proportion to the whole Gospel. There is not the mere fact that we do not know when Jesus was born, but in the early church, in the earliest proclamation of the Gospel, indeed, in the whole New Testament, the center of gravity, the chief focus was not Christmas. In fact, there is no Christmas in the New Testament in the sense of a great festival in the church. There are, of course, in two Gospels the stories of Jesus' birth, but the rest of the New Testament is not concerned about details surrounding Jesus' birth, but rather of the meaning of his ministry, his appearance as a full-grown adult, and his mission that became manifest in the cross and resurrection. Not Christmas, but Good Friday and Easter form the focus of the New Testament Gospel. The salvation event that was preached after Pentecost dealt with the drama of Jesus' suffering, his death and his exaltation. The Christ of Calvary and the Christ of Easter occupy the center of the stage in the faith of the early church. The stories of Jesus, the child of Bethlehem, enter in at a later stage, and then are made to serve as a kind of poetic preamble, as a beautiful overture to the main theme of atonement and resurrection. This is not to minimize Christmas, but it is to slow down the locomotive of tradition, which has a tendency at times to stop too long at the minor stations, and not long enough at the major ones. The key event is the rising of the crucified Jesus from death unto life. And that ought to be observed in the structure, in the tempo, and in the emphasis in our faith and church calendar.

I would not join the chorus of those who say that Christmas is a pagan festival; let's get rid of it; or that it has been secularized beyond recovery. It not only has pagan parallels, but it has always had pagan overtones. If our secular culture can make something humanly enjoyable and even commercially profitable out of the last days of December, we do not need to be grumpy about that. There is no reason why a secular holiday and the worship of Christ the Savior cannot go together, if we know which is which.

2. THE MEANING OF THE MYTH AND REALITY OF SALVATION

The second observation has to do with whether the incarnation is a myth that we can still believe with a good conscience. We should not let ourselves be beguiled by the word *myth*. There are myths which are merely the cunningly devised fables which St. Paul says that we ought to avoid. Our ordinary language implies that a myth is a fiction, a fairy tale which is not to be taken seriously. But there are words which have several meanings. The word *myth* also has the meaning of a story in which the Eternal is portrayed in human terms, in which the otherworldly is described in terms of this world, in which the word and the will of God are portrayed in events which happen in time and space. In this latter sense, in this special sense, of the eternal God manifesting himself in the form of a man on earth, the features of the mythical narrative form are obvious.

But the final question is not what you call it — it is not the literary type or narrative form that is of ultimate importance. Who of us could say that God can reveal himself only in one or two types of human expression? If God is to reveal himself, he reveals himself in ways which a human being can understand. Who would limit God as to the forms through which he can reveal his will and love to mankind? The real question then is whether there is a significant reality or event which is transparent through the literary form. Is there a significant reality, is there truth, is there saving power and meaning in the stories? To get at that truth, that reality, that saving power and meaning does not mean that we take every story, every detail literally, in terms of objective historical facts. The expressive form and the saving mystery cannot be confused or identified; neither should they be separated and torn apart. The stories of the birth of Jesus are incomparable; they cannot be replaced; we need them in order to convey the depth of the mystery of omnipotent Love entering into the stream of earthly existence.

Profound mysteries can never be literally expressed in human language. What God has done in Jesus Christ is so utterly new and unique that human language is stretched to the bursting point. Factual descriptions must cease and blend into the language of praise, into symbols of imagination, into the doxology of the heart. We must be at home in the language of images, of the imagination, symbols, and myth, for the mystery we proclaim is reality which transcends the ordinary words we use to talk about ordinary things. Thus we can and must say if the Eternal Word has become flesh, if the Eternal King has appeared as a lowly servant to save us, if Jesus is Immanuel, the God who is on our side, then we also expect all the resources of loving imagination, of creative intuition, of poetic feeling to be employed in giving unforgettable and lasting expression to this marvelous event. This is no event for the mere chronicler who with his physical eyes slantedly picks out mere surface facts and sequences of cause and effect. Let the poet and the hymn writers and the sober preachers of parables find the fitting words in which to enshrine the eternal meaning in frail and fragile words. Let us then speak of shepherds and angels, of wise men and the moving star, of the holy family and the Virgin Birth. Let us do so if we have the imagination to use such language, and if we can keep our eyes on the Savior, who is the center of attraction.

3. THE VIRGIN BIRTH

Then we come to our third point: the birth of Jesus from Mary the Virgin. It is a fact that neither Paul nor John mention one word about any Virgin Birth. It could not have been uppermost. It is a fact that the earliest sermons of the apostles recorded in Acts do not mention one word about the Virgin Birth. It is also a fact that many modern listeners of the Gospel take offense at this idea. What are we to do? Shall we remain silent in order not to offend anyone? You know how quick we are to recall the words that the preaching of the Gospel is foolishness to the Greeks and a stumbling block to the Jew. We know that we cannot avoid the preaching of the scandal, let the chips fall where they may. We must be honest enough to remember that this foolishness, this stumbling block, this scandal which the Apostles spoke of had to do, not with Christmas or Bethlehem or the Virgin Birth, but with the cross and the resurrection. If we are to be faithful preachers, we cannot transpose or shift this scandal to some other point. We cannot say the Virgin Birth is *the* scandal. We cannot say that it comprises the heart of the Gospel. Preaching which calls men to decision, to repentance and faith in face of the living God, whose judgment and grace are enacted in the living Christ, cannot make belief in the Virgin Birth a binding condition of faith in the Savior.

On the other hand, the birth stories serve a real purpose. They have meaning to those who are already in communion with the living Christ. They are not part of the missionary proclamation as such; rather, they are ways of expressing the conviction of faith that Jesus, our Lord, is no ordinary human being; he cannot be explained in terms of heredity and environment. He is a full member of the human race; his mother is a human being, and yet he brings to the human race what that race cannot achieve for itself. He is the bringer of salvation. He is conceived by the Holy Spirit. He is the

Word made flesh. He is flesh of our flesh and bone of our bone, and yet he is the visible expression of the invisible God.

The story of the Virgin Birth describes the event of salvation *by grace alone*. It expresses that the life of Jesus is not only in the likeness of men, but that he comes forth from God. Unto us is born a Savior. The Virgin Birth marks off the mystery of his birth, just as the empty tomb marks off the victorious close of the life of Jesus. In the Virgin Birth, Christians believe, God has vindicated his sovereignty; he has shown that he alone is master and Lord. Humanity cannot take credit for Jesus. Our culture produces great men. But it cannot account for Jesus. He is the One in whom God has acted. He is the work of God. That is what we mean when we say that he was conceived by the Holy Ghost.

The story of the Virgin Birth is a sacred treasure of the Christian faith and not laboratory data for biologists who experiment with parthenogenesis. Let no one treat the Virgin Birth as if he holds a club in his hand by which to hit people over the head. Let it be expounded to those who already believe in Christ as Lord and Savior, and not make it a hurdle or an obstacle to faith. Let us be wise as serpents and gentle as doves. Let us not handle the glad tidings as if we were throwing stones at people's heads.

4. THE MEANING OF CHRISTMAS

Our fourth and final point has to do with the meaning of the Christmas miracle for our lives. What does Christmas, the message of the incarnation, mean for our existence? If the Christmas stories are only beautiful pictures, to entertain our minds and to appeal to aesthetic appetites, if they do not speak to our urgent questions, impinging on the facts of sin and guilt, tragedy and loneliness, the need to have and to belong, if these stories do not meet us where our hearts ache, in the heartbeats of hope, in the pathos of our suffering, in the clamor for political freedom, in the filthiness of racial hate, across the barriers of suspicion and mistrust, then we have no right to waste the time of our fellowmen with quaint myths which only sound like stories of the shenanigans and horseplay of Olympian deities. We do not believe in the antics of the primitive God. Our God is the Father of our Lord Jesus Christ who was not playing around, but was entering into the serious and urgent business of living within the conditions of human life. He took the form of a servant, lived in humble obedience to the will of God, and plunged himself into a life-and-death struggle with the powers of personal and social and cosmic evil.

I believe, therefore, that it ought to be a primary rule of our Christian thinking: never be satisfied to stop short of discovering the meaning of a text for human existence; always to show how the message is related to the problems of life. Only then can we prevent our doctrines from being irrelevant and boring. Simply to recite stories, or to make statements that are biblical and orthodox is not to preach the gospel. Preaching the gospel of the incarnation means to find the roots of meaning and the hidden reality in the stories that have to do with the concerns of human existence, of human community. Our struggling, agonizing history is in search of meaning and ultimate redemption which the future course of history cannot produce out of itself. The history of Jesus Christ, in whom God has come, discloses the goal and meaning of all history, bringing the answer to the human predicament. The mystery of the incarnation is the mystery of suffering love in the midst of evil in the world, assuaging man's thirst for freedom, his search for authentic life lived in love and true community, giving hope that will not be conquered by the bleak horror of a nation's tragedy, social frustration, personal despair, and international strife. The Christmas stories affirm the participation of God in human estrangement, in the struggles of history, in the sores of society, in the bleeding wounds of human hearts. We must preach these stories with all conviction, in the fullness of the biblical picture, making transparent the majesty of God in the lowly figure of Jesus the servant, who shares with us in the misery of humanity.

Part Two

The Whole
Gospel

8

The Righteousness of God and the Rights of Man

Rom. 3:21-27: "But now the righteousness of God has been manifested apart from law, although the law and the prophets bear witness to it, the righteousness of God through faith in Jesus Christ for all who believe. For there is no distinction; since all have sinned and fall short of the glory of God, they are justified by his grace as a gift, through the redemption which is in Christ Jesus, whom God put forward as an expiation by his blood, to be received by faith. This was to show God's righteousness, because in his divine forbearance he had passed over former sins; it was to prove at the present time that he himself is righteous and that he justified him who has faith in Jesus.

"Then what becomes of our boasting? It is excluded. On what principle? On the principle of works? No, but on the principle of faith."

The righteousness of God — this is what the Reformation was all about. Justification is a weaker word for the same thing. In Luther's time there were many who viewed the righteousness of God as the backbone of law and order, only pushed to divine infinity. The demand of God's righteousness was for an increase of law and the obedient pursuit of a religion of established order, religious duties, canonical legalities, revealed authorities, and properly instituted channels of grace. Grace was seen as God's power to meet the demands of the law, to brace the individual in his striving to reach the high righteousness of God. It is not a moral attribute of God; it is surely not a way of putting God on the side of law and order. Nor is it God's perfect moral sense aligning his prestige with the custodians of law and the values of the established system. Käsemann has said that the righteousness of God is not a divine attribute; that it is a misconception of Greek theology. God's righteousness is instead a power. It is power to stir things up, to shatter imprisoning conventions. It is manifest beyond law and order as power to blaze new trials of freedom and life.

Jesus anticipated the reign of righteousness from the advancing reality of God's kingdom. When the kingdom of God comes, it brings righteousness. This righteousness seeks the rights of man, for it cares for human integrity. It puts things right between persons, for it cares for reconciling peace to rule all their relationships. It makes things right between men and God, because it leads to the fullness of life in the freedom of God. God's righteousness is the power of God in relation to people who are not in the right, who do not do what is right, who violate the rights of others in self-righteous aggression, who rob God of his rights and of his due, by putting him down in their pride.

Does that mean God has no use for law? By no means. Law is a necessary evil that God has to use to pressure people to do what is right, to give others their due, even when unrighteous people are not motivated by the righteousness of God. The power of God uses the pressure of law to hold things together until the future brings in a new wave of freedom and righteousness. Laws are good when, in holding things together, they do not become rigid and inflexibly opposed to new things and new dimensions of justice and love. Laws are evil and unjust when they freeze the present in the interests of the rich, at the bitter expense of the poor.

The law cannot be a way of salvation, our reforming fathers said, because those who serve it most eagerly are inflated by their own righteousness. They apply the law to constrict the rights of lowly men. Therefore, Jesus entered into conflict not with the lawless but precisely with the custodians of the law. Jesus' fight was against the lawlessness of law because he stood for the transcendent righteousness of God. When the law becomes lawless, righteous men become revolutionary.

The righteousness which God brings is revealed in Christ as a gift of pure love. The righteousness of God is fullness of life, and that life is to be found in Jesus because he represented fully the righteousness of God by exploring the fullness of life for others. For that cause he died. Jesus is the representative of both God and man by his living and dying for others. God accepts those who enter into his future with the representative righteousness of Christ. Here is the heartland of the Reformation. On account of Christ we are declared righteous. By grace we are justified through faith, and not by the works of the law.

Some of us may have given up on these great Reformation slogans. Perhaps there is in part the ecumenical urge, in part also sheer fatigue in the face of worn-out slogans. A few will say that the message of justification is irrelevant to modern man; modern man is not asking about a gracious God, but whether God exists at all. There can be little doubt that the juridical language about justification does not ring any bells in modern ears. So let us for a while stop speaking of justification. Instead, let us catch up to those who speak about the rights of men, who seek a righteous society. Many of our contemporaries are in desperate earnestness about righteousness. If people in the church do not care about righteousness, others will. Justification language may be dull; but language about righteousness is exciting. Are we not crusading for the rights of man? We are always demanding our rights. We want to be in the right, so we try to prove others in the wrong; then we become victims of self-righteousness. We are quick to see through hypocrisy and self-righteous claims, especially those of others, but not our own. There are men in earnest seeking to do what is right. That is good news for today. For if all we had was the righteousness that is manifest through law as we know it, we would be in a terrible fix.

The righteousness of God in Christ is good news; he has given us a signature in blood affixed to the promise that the rights and the rightness of man will be established in the end. The righteousness of Christ frees us from having to prove our own rightness; it liberates us to seek instead the rights of others. "It is an edifying thought," Søren Kierkegaard said, "to know that before God I am always in the wrong." It is good to have this one thing clear. Therefore, the righteousness of God is not a standard to which I must attain through a religion of law and a politics of order. It is a power of God beyond the law to bring future salvation to men in the present, so they can act from freedom and not from fear, so they can open up life to future realities, and not keep it imprisoned in the space that is patrolled by the repressive instruments of law and order. The righteousness of God is not concerned with how people can serve law and order, but rather with how law and order can serve the rights of men on their way to a righteousness that will endure forever.

The righteousness of God is a power that grasps us, not a property we can possess. The gift of righteousness in Christ places us on the road that drives through the world back to God. Righteousness is grace for the world, not a warm feeling inside of being a good Christian. This gift is given us in such a way that we have it only as something that lies ahead of us. Paul says, "We wait for the hope of righteousness." God's gift of righteousness to the world in Christ is like opening an account on which travelers can draw as they spend their life in a country far from home. They live in trust that the notes are good. Only in the end will they know for sure whether the notes have been backed by gold. Meanwhile, faith is both believing they are good and spending the notes with confidence, putting faith in the One who has signed the notes

with his life and death. The gift of righteousness now
announces a goal that is still future for each individual and
the world. The person who thinks he has already crossed that
goal, who acts like he has already arrived, is a pathetic figure.
Such an illusion leads to a perfectionist boasting, generating
hypocrisy in the individual and triumphalism in the church.

God's righteousness reveals the world as in need of a new
Lord. The resurrection of Jesus — what else is it but the
enthronement of Jesus to Lordship? For the world this
means a chance for change, a new leadership, a new loyalty, a
new goal. For us as individuals it means to let the power of
God's rule create a new obedience in our bodies and a new
loyalty in our minds. For the church it means new tongues
and a new song, to proclaim to the world the news of its
inheritance of freedom, life, and shalom calling us to celebrate right now the joy of life that has burst upon us. By
grace each day is a new departure into the untrammeled
future of life. In accepting God's decision for us on account
of Christ, in accepting the alien righteousness of Christ, we
let this suffice for our own future, and in this we find freedom to live now for others. God receives our service of
righteousness only as we pour it through the world back into
him.

As true sons of the Reformation let us go forward with the
hope of righteousness that lets freedom ring and brings the
pulse beats of truth and of joy into the stream of our life.

9

To Stand

or to

Fall

Rom. 3:21-28: "But now the righteousness of God
has been manifested apart from law, although the law
and the prophets bear witness to it, the righteousness
of God through faith in Jesus Christ for all who
believe. For there is no distinction; since all have
sinned and fall short of the glory of God, they are
justified by his grace as a gift, through the redemption which is in Christ Jesus, whom God put forward
as an expiation by his blood, to be received by faith.
This was to show God's righteousness, because in his
divine forbearance he had passed over former sins; it
was to prove at the present time that he himself is
righteous and that he justifies him who has faith in
Jesus.

"Then what becomes of our boasting? It is excluded. On what principle? On the principle of
works? No, but on the principle of faith."

Have you read the message from the fourth assembly of
the Lutheran World Federation in Helsinki? The Helsinki
delegates worked long and hard to draft a new statement on
justification by grace through faith, a statement which might
have the double advantage of being true to that article of
faith, rediscovered by Martin Luther, by which the church
stands or falls and of being relevant to the existence of
modern man who himself is daily at the brink of standing or
falling. It is not our purpose to offer a full-scale evaluation of

whether the delegates succeeded or failed. It is not even our purpose to take sides in that tug of war between those who stressed the new existential questions of the twentieth century.

But one thing was said at Helsinki which must cause us to ponder very seriously. The Helsinki message said: "The man of today no longer asks, 'How can I find a gracious God?' His question is more radical, more elementary: he asks about God as such, 'Where is God?' He suffers not from God's wrath, but from the impression of his absence; not from sin, but from the meaninglessness of his own existence; he asks not about a gracious God, but whether God really exists."

There you have it! The man in Luther's time, and indeed Luther himself, did not ask, "Is there a God?" But rather, "Is God really gracious; does God love us enough to save us?" So we are told by the Helsinki assembly and from many other quarters that the question of modern man is much more radical, our burdens much greater, our problems more profound. Therefore, presumably we need a more radical answer to meet the challenge of our more radical questions. Many of us have been wondering whether the Reformation message of justification is still powerful enough to deal with the radical questions of twentieth-century man.

In the volume on reconciliation of his *Church Dogmatics*, Karl Barth wrote the following words ten years before the Lutheran mecca to Helsinki: "Of all the superficial catchwords of our age, surely one of the most superficial is that, whereas sixteenth-century man was concerned about the grace of God, modern man is much more radically concerned about God himself as such . . . that is, whether God exists at all."

Karl Barth is right. That *is* a superficial catchword, because modern man is not seriously interested in the idle question, to be debated at his leisure, whether God does or does not exist. But modern man is profoundly concerned about certain age-old questions, which are not answered simply by assuring him that there really is a God. The most radical answer to man's question is not that there is a God. That, taken by itself, turns out to be an empty, frivolous and irrelevant thing to say or to believe. The really radical answer to modern man's question must be one which concerns the standing or falling of man himself. This would be the answer to the question of salvation. Any talk about God's existence that is not linked to the question of man's salvation is superficial talk. Only armchair philosophers and somewhat confused theologians have time for such idle chatter. The basic question of man in all ages is the question of the meaning of existence. There are many aspects to this question. They have taken various shapes in the heart of man as long as man has been man. The struggle for love, the quest for power, the sense of guilt, and the encounter with death — all aspects of man's search for meaning and salvation in this life and forever. Am I accepted by others? Does my life have worth? Am I free from an accusing conscience and the unrelieved pain in the hell of life, from the condemnation of guilt? If a man die, shall he live again? Who can deliver me from this body of death? Is there a righteousness apart from the law? That means, is there any way out of this bondage to the law which restricts me, warps me, produces fanaticism, illusions, and pride, and from which I incur a sickness of personality so serious that my hatred of others is exceeded only by self-estrangement.

There is but one solid answer to these questions. The answer is not merely that there is a God somewhere. It is rather that there is a gracious God, a God who cares, who has revealed his saving righteousness. The modern question about the existence of God and Luther's quest for a gracious God are not two unrelated things. At bottom they are grounded in the same concern.

In Samuel Beckett's play, *Waiting for Godot*, we see how modern man himself connects the question of God's existence to the question of salvation. Estragon and Vladimir are waiting for someone they call Godot. They have no clear idea about who Godot is, but they sense the meaninglessness of their own existence. At the end of the play they have looked for Godot in vain. If only Godot would come, things would be different. Then they say, "We'll hang ourselves tomorrow . . . .Unless Godot comes. And if he comes? Why, then we'll be saved." But Godot does not come! The curtain falls upon their despair. Knowing that Godot existed somewhere did not relieve their despair — but if only Godot would come, he would save them.

As believers in Christ we do a foolish thing if we dangle before men the tantalizing question whether God exists. Modern man has lost interest in that as a debatable question. The situation is perhaps quite the reverse of what Helsinki's message says. Man is not so much interested in the question of God's existence as such. Many modern men could not care less. But people today are concerned about whether the meaning of life can be affirmed, whether there is a saving power which overcomes futility, obscenity, and bestiality, whether the homesickness and restlessness of man can be cured.

Man has had a horrifying revelation of himself in the twentieth century. The world wars, the concentration camps, the use of science and technology to create instruments of total destruction have brought about a collapse of the utopias which nineteenth-century man hoped to realize on earth. With the utopias gone, and with man's faith in himself destroyed, he hardly dares to hope, afraid to set his hopes too high, lest the last disappointment be more tragic than the first.

St. Paul's message in Romans and Luther's message in the sixteenth century do not tell us that there is a God who really exists. That is small comfort. Theirs is a much more radical message which brings the righteousness for which we are hungering and thirsting, not our own moral righteousness, but the verdict of God that because of Jesus Christ we are made acceptably righteous. This righteousness, which God has revealed in Jesus Christ, is not a graduated law of perfection which we can achieve. It is a free gift of grace; it is total, absolute, and unconditional. It is something that God gives, and which we receive through faith.

This righteousness is the verdict of God which removes the guillotine of guilt that hangs over us. It removes the death sentence pronounced upon us. It deals with the sin that separates us from God. This verdict of God in Jesus Christ decides whether in the end we shall stand upright or fall into the abyss of meaninglessness. The basic question that we ask today is the old question whether a person will stand or fall in the end. And by what power, by the energy of what reality can a person carry through to victory in a world shaken by transgressions and offenses and errors and follies and lies and faults and crimes against God, his creatures, and the earth on which they live?

What we need to know today is not whether God exists. We need to know the verdict of God in Jesus Christ. We offer stones instead of bread to our fellowmen if we separate the question of whether God exists from the question of God's verdict in Jesus Christ. The verdict of God has fallen once and for all in Jesus Christ. It is a final verdict that never needs to be reenacted. It is valid for all time. We are called to hear and rejoice in that verdict. St. Paul spoke of that verdict of God when he preached about righteousness, reconciliation, and justification. Luther in all essentials spoke of the same verdict when he stressed that the message of justification is the summary of the whole gospel by which the church stands or falls, and not only the church, but the whole world.

The verdict of God took place in the dying and rising of Jesus Christ. It has two sides: the verdict of death and the verdict unto new life. Jesus Christ took upon himself the death sentence. The man of Golgotha was taken down from the cross and was buried, and with him was buried God's contempt for the sinner. Man the sinner, the rebel against God, has gone down to defeat. He has ended in the grave. The innocent man, Jesus Christ, became the sinner in the eyes of God. All human crimes are bound up in the death of Jesus Christ. The other side of the verdict, the positive side, is that a new humanity has been created through death and has been brought into existence with the rising of Jesus from the grave. A new decree of God, a new act of the Creator, has brought new life into the world, the power of love, the possibility of reconciliation among segregated men, and a new birth of freedom. Henceforth, the future of man is a future of freedom. "If the Son shall make you free, you are free indeed."

The verdict of God is one hundred percent his work in the career and destiny of the man Jesus Christ. A Christian is simply one who has heard that verdict, has accepted it for himself, and joins the revolution which that engenders. God's verdict which has fallen in Jesus Christ is the decision on which the Christian stands. It is the adjudication of the judge. He stands on nothing else. Of course, there are many things on which we try to stand to evade the verdict of God. The verdict of God is an offense to us because we like to believe in the illusion of our innocence. The pious Jew believed that he could stand on the law. Medieval man believed that he could stand on meritorious works prescribed by a church that had taken it into its own hands to mete out salvation by degrees, and in proportion to merits earned. Today, modern man is either banking on the remaining assets of a shallow humanism or is slipping into a desperate nihilism; or because man cannot live on nothing, he cannot live in a vacuum, he is selling his soul to some new myths and ideologies. The good news of God's final verdict in Jesus Christ brings the same alternative to ancient, medieval, or modern, or post-modern man. It is the alternative of standing victoriously on the granite foundation of the verdict of God or of falling and sinking into bottomless oblivion.

To stand on the verdict of God, as Paul says, puts an end to all boasting and to all human strategies of salvation. This means that the church itself has nothing of which to boast. More particularly it means that Christians are not to boast before God or man of any peculiarity which they prize. The article of justification, which Luther rediscovered, is not the

monopoly of a particular church. It belongs to the foundation of the whole Christian church, because this article is no
mere theological idea alongside other interesting ideas. It
points rather to the verdict of God in Jesus Christ, which is
the charter and constitution of the Christian church signed
and authorized by the blood of Jesus the Christ. This article
of justification is not merely an ingredient in one denomination of Christianity. It is not a mere idiosyncrasy which one
church has to contribute to enrich the ecumenical potpourri,
as Anglicans contribute a taste for the liturgy, Eastern
Orthodoxy a mystical sense, Presbyterians a church discipline, Congregationalists a democratic polity, Roman Cath-
olicism an appreciation of order and authority in the church,
and so on. No, the article of justification by grace alone
through faith alone is that by which the whole church stands
or falls, even though the very terms are not used as such (the
term is not in the Catechisms at all), because that article
decides whether we stand on the verdict of God in Jesus
Christ, or whether we stand on ourselves, and thereby fall
into boasting, bringing misery and judgment upon ourselves,
by nullifying the death and resurrection of Jesus Christ.

   We stand at a crossroads today as churches confront each
other in the ecumenical movement. The whole movement is
threatened by the possibility of a deadening stalemate, as we
simply look at each other and possibly tolerate each other's
traditions. The whole movement ends in a stalemate if we
only compare the way in which our various traditions look at
Christ. For this is finally only a subtle form of boasting,
resting on ourselves and boasting of our traditions, each one
as glorious and scandalous as the other. So what we need is a
new breakthrough of the Spirit of God, where we have the
insight and the courage to look at our traditions in the light
of God's verdict in Jesus Christ, a new act of the Spirit which
liberates Christ from the prison of traditions in which we
confine him. Christ is the Lord and the Judge of our traditions, even of those most precious traditions which have been
created to his glory and honor in the past.

A Reformation Day celebration may be a blessed thing if it is not simply a kind of alumni day, a cozy rendezvous for self-flattery and tradition-mongering, satisfying ourselves in the act of adulating Luther, the hero of our tradition. It may be a blessed thing if we can hear the verdict of God, if the church responds to the call to stand exclusively upon its foundation, the righteousness of God and the redemption in Jesus Christ. This is so important, for the church exists for the world, and whether the world shall stand or fall is equally decided by the verdict of God in Jesus Christ. The world today needs to hear that verdict. What we have heard we must also proclaim.

10

The Voice

of the

Law

Rom. 3:19-31: "Now we know that whatever the law says it speaks to those who are under the law, so that every mouth may be stopped, and the whole world may be held accountable to God. For no human being will be justified in his sight by works of the law, since through the law comes knowledge of sin.

"But now the righteousness of God has been manifested apart from law, although the law and prophets bear witness to it, the righteousness of God through faith in Jesus Christ for all who believe. For there is no distinction; since all have sinned and fall short of the glory of God, they are justified by his grace as a gift, through the redemption which is in Christ Jesus, whom God put forward as an expiation by his blood, to be received by faith. This was to show God's righteousness, because in his divine forbearance he had passed over former sins; it was to prove at the present time that he himself is righteous and that he justifies him who has faith in Jesus.

"Then what becomes of our boasting? It is excluded. On what principle? On the principle of works? No, but on the principle of faith. For we hold that a man is justified by faith apart from works of law. Or is God the God of Jews only? Is he not the God of Gentiles also? Yes, of Gentiles also, since God is one; and he will justify the circumcised on the ground of their faith and the uncircumcised because of their faith. Do we then overthrow the law by this faith? By no means! On the contrary, we uphold the law."

There is a new book on Lutherans in America. It is called *A Study of Generations* — a very large and expensive book. It comes out with a conclusion that we had always suspected, because we have been living with ourselves all our lives. The conclusion is that there are gospel-oriented Lutherans and law-oriented Lutherans (the same dichotomy might prove true of any other group). Some are more one than the other and some are fifty-fifty. Of course, this was anything but an unprejudiced and value-free study. The authors are themselves Lutherans and are committed to the reality of the law-and-gospel scheme as the most valid way of interpreting both the revelation of God and the experience of man. I am not going to give a critical review of their report on Lutherans, though that should come in due time. But since this is the latest word from Lutherans about law and gospel, and since Luther drew his ideas about law and gospel out of his own reading of Romans and Galatians, it is well that we expose this modern prestigious study of Lutherans to Paul's own preaching on the law.

The picture of a law-oriented Lutheran is that he cannot stand change; he is an absolutist, filled with prejudice, somewhat of a racist. He is a literalist and a fundamentalist. In short, he is hooked on what St. Paul calls salvation by the works of the law. We all know that we cannot be justified by the works of the law, so in the end we are not given much hope for these law-oriented Lutherans. They are the worst kind.

Then we turn to this other category of people, the gospel-oriented Lutherans, and suddenly we feel more at home with the good guys in the white hats. It is obvious that these authors prefer this type; not in so many words of self-praising and self-congratulation would we or the authors count ourselves among this type, but if you come right out and ask us if we are the gospel-oriented Lutherans, we would of course have to admit it. We are gospel-oriented Lutherans! We do not believe in salvation by works. We have a whole profile of such a gospel-orientation, and it looks very much like Paul's description of the Pharisee. Now Paul did not dislike the Pharisee; he was one himself. Look at what a fine Pharisee a gospel-oriented Lutheran is! First of all, he is neither a liberal nor a fundamentalist; but he is a conservative, leaning just a little bit toward the side of the progressives in social matters. He holds a balanced view of the Trinity, so that God is evenly transcendent and immanent. He believes in justification by faith alone and rejects works-righteousness. This gospel-oriented Lutheran has warm feelings about worship, prayer, and personal faith. Such Lutherans believe in the divinity of Jesus, in the Bible as God's word, and other items on a long list of approved beliefs, attitudes, values, and behavior patterns, according to what we regard as best in the Lutheran tradition.

So we have two types of Lutherans after all, according to this study, the good guys and the bad guys. Of course, there is a little bit of bad in all of us, and a little bit of good in the worst of us. So we are told. The gospel-oriented Lutherans look pretty good; they look pretty much like our own image of ourselves.

Then what becomes of our boasting? What is St. Paul's point in Romans 3? His point is that gospel-oriented Lutherans may be the best kind, but they are not going to make it that way. Pharisees are not going to make it. Anyone who measures up, by any chique list of fitting rules and approved categories, is not going to make it. Does God show mercy on the gospel-oriented Lutherans? Is not this new list of correct credentials but another ladder that invites us to climb to heaven, with each rung of our own righteousness taking us higher and higher? By so doing we make another law out of gospel-talk. We find out what the gospel says, and we turn it into a law, into a ladder that we can climb. When we reach the top, we congratulate ourselves, assuming that it goes without saying that we gospel-oriented Lutherans are better and more pleasing to God and our fellowmen, and more free and useful than law-oriented Lutherans.

For there is no distinction. If you make a list of attributes, and back it up with empirical data scientifically established, and play that list off against another list, there still is no distinction. For we have all sinned and we all fall short. Those who say that there is a distinction are thinking according to the law and are measuring the works of the law — which is the only thing you can measure. So some are good, some are better, and some are really bad. But about those who in the name of the superiority of the gospel make such a distinction, Paul says, "Their throat is an open grave; they use their tongues to deceive." They are under the judgment of the law and are found to be sinners, like everyone else. There is a profound solidarity in sin between law-oriented and gospel-oriented Christians. There is no ground for boasting. For both are justified by God's grace as a gift, through the one redemption which is in Christ Jesus. This is no feather in anyone's cap, no prize for anyone's trophy case, not something that can be put on display, to put the others down and to build ourselves up. Jesus would have said about this, it is impossible for a gospel-oriented Lutheran to enter the kingdom of God. Why? Because he is so obviously better off than the law-oriented Lutheran, he thinks he has got it made. He is standing on his credentials, on pride in his doctrines, his beliefs, his attitudes, his values, which are all of the right kind of course, according to the law of our tradition.

In the light of the message of Romans, law-oriented and gospel-oriented Christians are very much alike beneath the skin. If you scratch deep enough, they both bleed the same way. If you attack their pride, they both snap back the same. When their airplane falls out of the sky, both get hurt the same way. There is not that much difference, and before God there is no difference at all. This is what Paul was trying to say is the true value of the law, to drive home that point and to open us to the new basis of life. This is not a doctrine, not a belief, not a behavior pattern, but God's own decision, his own action, his own gospel, his own word of grace, his own coming, which we can never convert into our possession, put under our control, and flaunt in the face of these poor, miserable, bigoted, racist, biblically literalistic, and doctrinally fundamentalistic Lutherans, which on a purely human level I do not count among the friends I cherish the most. But my standards and your standards are not the law of God; for, like the gospel, he does not turn that over to us to manipulate in our favor. Before that law, there is no distinction, and we all have fallen short. Before that law our favorite kind of Lutheran, like the Jew in Romans 3, may have some advantage; something precious may have been entrusted to him, but he is no better, not at all.

This is the true value of the law; it levels us down, keeps us together, making us walk the same paths of ruin and misery, seeking and looking ahead toward the same peace and the same grace which God in Christ gives to both Jews and Gentiles, both law- and gospel-oriented people.

11

On

Evangelism

Matt. 28:19: "Go therefore and make disciples of all nations, baptizing them in the name of the Father and of the Son and of the Holy Spirit. . . ."

When one of the American astronauts landed on the moon, President Nixon exclaimed that it's the greatest event since the beginning of creation. His preacher-friend, Billy Graham, chided him and said, "No, Jesus Christ is the greatest event since the creation of the world." I read in the newspaper where a spokesman for Key 73 emphatically stated that this evangelistic crusade would be the greatest event in the history of Christianity. To that kind of PR I have to say, "We are off to a poor start." The advance publicity, the big strategies, and the triumphalist mentality behind such evangelistic ballyhoo might very well threaten to make this campaign one of the biggest fiascos in modern church history. And what if that is true? What if that really turns out to be the case? Some might take that gleefully as an excuse to forget about evangelism. They might say, "See there, evangelism is old hat, and doesn't work anymore. It's no longer the business of the church."

I want to remind you of one indispensable plank in the church's apostolic charter and constitution: the man Jesus from Nazareth said, "Go therefore and make disciples of all nations, baptizing them in the name of the Father and of the Son and of the Holy Spirit." Evangelism in the Christian church is pure and simply preaching the gospel of Jesus

Christ as the power of salvation for all mankind, and especially for those who do not yet believe. Evangelism is the church turning toward the world, that is, in the same direction in which God himself was turning in the personal posture of Jesus Christ. When the church lives closest to Jesus Christ, she also lives closest to the world, because Jesus is God's Man for this world.

Jesus called rather ordinary men to become first disciples and then apostles — men and women sent into the world to preach a compelling message of life to the dying and liberation to the captives. After Pentecost the apostles did not hang around Jerusalem, sitting at their desks in some bureau of apostolic affairs. In those days there were no bureaucrats in the church, keeping records to gather statistics to feed some hungry unbelieving computer. They were all busy at evangelism — that was the very spiritual breath of life and the life-blood flowing through the new body of which each person was a living member. This new body of theirs was not something they hid away in church, not like a light placed under a basket, or like a coin hid in the ground. They remembered that Jesus called them the salt of the earth, the light of the world, and the good seed sown in the field which is the world. As one theologian has put it: "The place for the salt is in the soup." The place for Christians is in the world, preaching the gospel to all nations, to all people.

But it is a risky thing for the church to do evangelism in the world. What if the church opens its mouth and has nothing to say? What if the church builds a terrific delivery system, but in the end nothing comes out of it but pious words and holy smoke? It is a bold and daring thing to launch an evangelistic campaign to "win the continent of North America for Christ," as the saying goes.

Is there such faith, such commitment to the gospel of Christ, such courage to bear the cross of Jesus on the part of the churches of North America that such an undertaking becomes really credible and promising? . . . in 1973?

All the more reason, in light of these warnings, that we in

the evangelical tradition take stock of the real state of affairs. If the church is to be the salt of the world, it must be salty. If it is to bring light, it must at least be a good reflector of a light brighter than itself. So what is the church to be and do at this time?

First, the church is called to bring the world to a new knowledge of itself. The Bible pictures the world as groping about in darkness; it announces the coming of a great light into the world — the light of Jesus the Christ.

Secondly, the church is to love God by converting that love into compassion for the world. It cannot be stated strongly enough that there is no way that our love for God can reach him in another world above this world. Our love for God can reach him only as we convert that love into concrete acts that serve the needs of our fellowmen.

It is indeed right that we link our evangelistic mission together with our social ministry. We had better not let evangelism become so much Pharisaic talking without some Samaritan acting to go along with it. There is such a thing as air pollution, water pollution, noise pollution; but there is also word pollution. For Jesus said, "It's not what goes into the mouth, but what comes out of it that defiles a man" and stinks up the atmosphere. As one whose profession is the right use of words, I shudder and tremble before the verbal avalanche that goes along with evangelistic campaigns, but I also hope and pray that there may be an outpouring of the Spirit to guide us in what to think and what to say.

Of course, I am not counseling silence. We have no choice. We are compelled; we feel constrained to preach the gospel. Woe is me, Paul said, if I preach not the gospel. Our primary task as the church in the world is not to be a political lobby, not to be a power structure, not to be a moralistic dictatorship, not to be a social agency, or philanthropic society doing good. Our primary task is to preach the word about Jesus, about God who has arrived with the power of his love and righteousness in that particular man Jesus. Our task is to attest to that word resolutely without looking to the right or to the left to see what kind of friends and fellow-travelers we have.

Because the word is our medium, we are in a dangerous situation. We are tempted to use words as does the modern world of commercial advertising and political propaganda — telling lies, covering up the truth, shrinking minds, stretching facts, and glossing over bitter realities. The church is tempted to drape itself in words of piety, to anoint itself with words of self-praise, and to indulge in programs of self-satisfaction and sterile in-breeding. We will not succeed in building a tower of Babel with words that can reach the ears of God in heaven. For God right now can only hear the wailing of women's voices who have lost their sons and husbands in wars; he can only hear the cries of little children who reach for breasts that give no milk; he can only hear the moanings of men who sit in prison shorn of dignity and in dreadful fear of brutality. It's not so much the prayers of the pious as the cries of the hopeless that God hears with his open heart of pain. In response to that cliché, "Does God answer prayers?" we can confidently say that, since God is like Jesus, he hears the cries of the homeless and the helpless and the hopeless. He is stretched out in pain for the least of all his brethren, for those who are lost and for those who are last.

Because this is where God is coming with his kingdom, because he is always concerned about a lost cause, the hunger for success that is bedeviling the church today is a godless urge. The church has been spared the obligation to succeed because its own Lord and Savior was a loser in this kind of world that respects chiefly the language of power, of military violence, of economic greed, and of sensual self-seeking. We are free to fail. If a particular evangelistic crusade promises a good old-fashioned American success story, it will run head-long against the one who said that "God did not spare his own son but delivered him up for us all." Accordingly, we shall not be spared tribulation, distress, persecution, even famine, nakedness, peril, or the sword . . . but in spite of all that, we have this promise, and that is all we have, that nothing can separate us from the love of God. It is a liberating thought to know as a minister and as a congregation that we do not have to succeed at all in whatever we try. We have only to be found faithful and obedient.

The worst form of success that we could have as a congregation is this: we could get lots of new members, all transferring from the world into the church without any basic change in themselves. What will happen is that not being changed themselves, they will surely change the church, remaking it into a pagan shrine. The trouble with Christianity in the West — in Europe and America — is not that there are too few church members; it is rather that there are teeming millions of them who have succeeded in so redefining what is Christian, that the church's faith is cut down to the size of the world's idealism. In Western Christianity it is hard to know what a person would have to believe and to do in order to be counted as something other than Christian. We have brought about a strange reversal. In New Testament times it was hard and costly to be a Christian. In today's times it is hard to be anything else.

It is not uncommon for the term *Christian* to mean something like having good intentions or trying hard to be a nice person. In getting lots of new members to add to an already inflated list of nominal Christians, who might, to be sure, help pay some of our secular bills, we might only succeed in speeding up the death of our congregations. Much more important than the quantity of people in the churches is the purity of faith to will that one thing, to cherish the pearl of great price, to be the people of Christ and of his cross in the world. "Do not be conformed to the world, but be ye transformed by the renewing of your minds."

More important then is the renewal of the people we already have in our churches. Along with outreach into the wider community must go a deeper spiritual penetration of that inner space of life, the inner life of each person, so that Jesus Christ might be preached not only by our words but also by our lives, visible for all to see.

We must go into every evangelistic effort with our theological heads screwed on right. That means not getting carried away by waves of emotion and thoughtless crusading for the loves and loyalties of people. We are heirs of a great theological heritage that should guide our preaching of the gospel. The Reformation church has doctrines of which we need not be ashamed. They can work to help us call the signals for the plays that unfold at the line of scrimmage. This theology of the gospel is not the gospel itself; it is like the system of numbers and letters that a good quarterback has at his command, which he barks out to his players, instructing them what to do. Here is the first signal: there is nothing that we can add to the gospel of salvation. The work is finished; in Christ there is always the complete revelation and salvation of God. Anything added to this is only rubbish and works-righteousness. In Jesus the kingdom of God and his rule of righteousness are fully revealed, so that we do not look for another savior and another salvation. We are the people who find their way, who confess the truth and experience life through Jesus our Lord.

The second signal is this: our only motive in evangelism, in breaking the news to the nations and all people who do not confess the name of Jesus, is to bring honor and glory to his name, and not to seek our own advantages or to be looking for any fringe benefits. This is a word of warning especially to those congregations which have become commercial enterprises, big business, as it were, lest they forget that Jesus was the man who kicked the money-changers out of the temple. A church that is involved in big business is a prime candidate to become a servant of the rule of Satan and his satellites. It is hard for the rich man — the rich church — to enter the kingdom of God. The temptation is severe to affluent and wealthy congregations.

Thirdly, we get this signal: build up the church, which is the body of Christ, through faithful worship, through serious education, through a responsible care of souls, rather than looking for instant Christians, quickie solutions, and magic gimickry to bring on spectacular results that do not survive under the heat of the sun. Be on your guard against the easy way, the quick result, the magic wand, the gala-gala man, the big promise, the huge success, the grand finale, the happy ending, the soothing story, and all those tempting tricks which the slick salesmen of a worldly church will sell for a few lousy bucks.

What this world needs now is a real church with a message of truth, the power of divine criticism, the courage of faith, the vision of hope, the actions of love, all of which need not add up to a big evangelistic campaign that will make glaring headlines in the secular press, but which will count infinitely for the kingdom of God. For there is more rejoicing in heaven for one sinner that repents, for one coin that is found, one sheep brought home safe, than for the ninety-nine that sit around in their safe and comfortable havens. In this spirit, with this kind of evangelical calculus and strange kingdom arithmetic we dare to move into another year of preaching and acting, to bring all things captive to Jesus Christ our Lord.

12

The

Book of

Promises

Isa. 11:1, 10: "There shall come forth a shoot from
the stump of Jesse, and a branch shall grow out of his
roots. . . . [which] shall stand as an ensign to the
peoples . . . ."

The ancient writings of the Hebrews contain many things
— myths and histories, laws and prophecies, poetry and
wisdom. But what is it about these Scriptures that still attract
us? I think it is their hopes for the future that still seem valid
today. The greatest force that ran through Israel and from
Israel out into the wider world was an image of the future
that had the power to keep each day fresh and free, an open
channel for hope. The great force was Yahweh, of whom no
image could be made. All of Yahweh's eminent rivals — all of
his competition — from Egypt, Canaan, Babylonia, Persia,
and Rome died a couple thousand years ago. Only Yahweh
lives, and the secret to his survival was that he was always
opening a new stretch of the road for his people to travel.

It was the forward look of Israel, the fact that Israel
awaited fulfillment from the future that kept her alert and
alive in history — in spite of all deviations and interim catas-
trophes. Someone has said that all of Israel's religious contemporaries were *spectators* on the world scene. Israel was a
listener and strained for the new word or a new twist on an
old word. The word was the instrument of prophetic tran-

scendence. It was the prophet's openness to the word of God that kept the people of Israel in motion from slavery in Egypt on the way to the Promised Land. It was the word that kept enlarging the vision of the future, for the word came not as an objective report, an obituary about the past, but as a promise for the future.

As twentieth-century men we are still looking for that future. We are still in a period of waiting, though the Lord has been good to bring us manna from heaven for our daily life, fragments of fulfillment along the way. The promises of God came through the prophets; but they are meant for all of us, because the promises lengthen and widen until they are universal in scope and eschatological in final validity. They are meant for all men for all time to come, so the Bible has become, as Lessing said, "the book of humanity."

The Bible is the book of humanity because the promises point ahead to our unfinished humanity, to the unfinished business of making human life truly human and a more perfect image of the fullness and freedom of God.

During this Advent season let the words of the prophets of Israel become portals of great hope; let them become a wreath of hope; let them make a radiant arch on the horizon of the coming of our Lord. For the prophets spoke of the remaking of the world, when those who hunger and thirst shall be fed; the rivers of water shall be pure, and there shall be enough bread and wine; the wilderness shall be glad and the desert shall blossom as a rose. Nature will be transfigured and man will receive a new spirit, the spirit of shalom. He will be stripped of his skin of selfishness and given a new body with instincts for righteousness.

Even the animal world will share in the reign of peace, so that the wolf shall dwell with the lamb, the leopard lie down with the kid, and the calf and the lion and the fatling together, and a little child shall lead them.

But especially we look for the newness of man. When will he get a new heart in place of the stony one? When will the eyes of the blind be opened and the ears of the deaf unstopped? When shall the lame be able to walk and tongues of the dumb make sweet music?

When will there be peace, and when will there be a ruler reigning in righteousness? When will swords be turned into ploughshares and spears into pruninghooks, so that nation shall not lift up sword against nation, and we will study war no more?

How did the prophets mean that their vision for Israel and its destiny in world history shall be fulfilled? As the chosen people they shall be a blessing to all the world. For salvation is of the Jews. Out of Israel there was to arise the focus of ultimate meaning for all mankind, the fulcrum of universal history. Israel, a tiny group of nomads, hungry children of the desert, a persecuted people dispersed through the world, shall nevertheless exceed other nations in glory, as Joseph exceeded in glory the brothers who sold him into slavery. From Israel, the prophets said, there shall be a beacon that beckons, a light that goes out to all the Gentiles. Isaiah says: "And there shall come forth a shoot out of the stump of Jesse, and a branch shall grow out of his roots. . . . [which] shall stand as an ensign to the peoples . . . ."

This and many other like promises make us all watchmen on the ramparts in history. While we wait we ask, "Where are the hopes of mankind fulfilled?" While we hope we pray for the glorious liberation of the children of God; and while we hope we work for the new life of righteousness to inhabit the world.

13

The

Apocalypse

of Hope

Rev. 7:1-17: "After this I saw four angels standing at
the four corners of the earth, holding back the four
winds of the earth, that no wind might blow on earth
or sea or against any tree. Then I saw another angel
ascend from the rising of the sun, with the seal of the
living God, and he called with a loud voice to the four
angels who had been given power to harm earth and
sea, saying, 'Do not harm the earth or the sea or the
trees, till we have sealed the servants of our God upon
their foreheads.' And I heard the number of the
sealed, a hundred and forty-four thousand sealed, out
of every tribe of the sons of Israel, twelve thousand
sealed out of the tribe of Judah, twelve thousand of
the tribe of Reuben, twelve thousand of the tribe of
Gad, twelve thousand of the tribe of Asher, twelve
thousand of the tribe of Naphtali, twelve thousand of
the tribe of Manasseh, twelve thousand of the tribe of
Simeon, twelve thousand of the tribe of Levi, twelve
thousand of the tribe of Issachar, twelve thousand of
the tribe of Zebulun, twelve thousand of the tribe of
Joseph, twelve thousand sealed out of the tribe of
Benjamin.

"After this I looked, and behold, a great multitude
which no man could number, from every nation,
from all tribes and peoples and tongues, standing
before the throne and before the Lamb, clothed in
white robes, with palm branches in their hands, and
crying out with a loud voice, 'Salvation belongs to
our God who sits upon the throne, and to the Lamb!'
And all the angels stood round the throne and round

the elders and the four living creatures, and they fell
on their faces before the throne and worshiped God,
saying 'Amen! Blessing and glory and wisdom and
thanksgiving and honor and power and might be to
our God for ever and ever! Amen.'

"Then one of the elders addressed me, saying 'Who
are these, clothed in white robes, and whence have
they come?' I said to him, 'Sir, you know.' And he
said to me, 'These are they who have come out of the
great tribulation; they have washed their robes and
made them white in the blood of the Lamb.

" 'Therefore are they before the throne
        of God,
    and serve him day and night
        within his temple;
    and he who sits upon the throne
        will shelter them with his presence.
They shall hunger no more, neither
        thirst any more;
    the sun shall not strike them, nor
        any scorching heat.
For the Lamb in the midst of the
        throne will be their shepherd,
    and he will guide them to springs
        of living water;
    and God will wipe away every tear
        from their eyes. ' "

Rev. 21:3-4: ". . . and I heard a great voice from the
throne saying, 'Behold, the dwelling of God is with
men. He will dwell with them, and they shall be his
people, and God himself will be with them; he will
wipe away every tear from their eyes, and death shall
be no more, neither shall there be mourning nor
crying nor pain any more, for the former things have
passed away.' "

We have read two portions from the apocalypse of John.
The word *apocalypse* means "revelation." John is giving us a
picture of his dreams. It is a dream concerning the future. It
is a dream of hope. I believe that All Saints' Day is not
merely, not even primarily, a time when we remember with

respect those who have died. There are many ways of honoring the dead. We have a tomb to the unknown soldier and many monuments to the great men of the past. What is the point of remembering those who have died? The crucial question is whether there is a hope for mankind which transcends the unfulfillment of the past and the tragedies of the present.

The eschatology of the New Testament is an answer to the human question of hope. To be human is to hope; a man who has ceased to hope has begun to die. For hope is what keeps life moving forward. We must understand the revelation of John as a bold answer to the human question whether there is anything to hope for beyond the limits of a life that is bound to die, a life in which we cannot escape from tears and pain and sickness and tragedy. The picture of the future which John describes would make no sense at all if there is no sense to hope.

But we must hope. If anyone lets the scales fall from his eyes and looks deeply into the human reality, he will see that the profoundest literature of mankind uses the nonempirical language of myth and utopia to deal with the hopes of man. Immanuel Kant, the German philosopher, said there are only three great questions: (1) What can I know? (2) What ought I to do? and (3) What may I hope? He saw that a fully human quest in life cannot be boiled down to a single question. 1 Cor. 13:13 has another way of saying the same thing: "In this life we have three great lasting qualities — faith, hope, and love." Faith is the dynamic toward knowledge, love the power of action, and hope is directed to the future. If we take away a man's future, we take away his freedom; and with that we have taken away his humanity.

But why does man hope? We do not hope for what we already possess, Romans 8 states. This means that the mission of hope in human existence is to remind us of a lack, of a plight or predicament in our life. If I am in captivity, my hope is bent on deliverance; if I am in darkness, I hope for light. When we hope, we are saying something about our sickness, our slavery, our alienation, our exile, and our bondage to death. In old-fashioned language, we hope for salvation. For salvation means bringing a man to a realization of the fullest potentialities of humanity. Hope is an SOS signal of distress. If a person thinks that everything is all right with himself, with his friends and family, with his community and nation, and with the whole world of which he is a part, then he need not hope. He is exempt from the life of hope. But he has become something less than a human being.

Today we learn from medical psychology how essential hope is. There is a mysterious connection between the power of a patient to hang on to life and his ability to hope. The loss of hope makes the recovery to health impossible; it even accelerates the time of death.

In fact, hopelessness is a form of death to those still living. Above the doorway to hell Dante inscribed the words: "Abandon hope, all ye who enter here." This could be turned around to read: "Those who enter here have abandoned hope." Perhaps hell could best be pictured as a state of absolute hopelessness.

The dynamic of hope searches for an adequate language. The struggle between religions, and the struggle between any religion at all and what is widely called secularism today, is the struggle between alternative forms of hope. Is there anything to hope for? The Marxist says, "Yes"; the Marxist answer is relevant to humanity because it responds to the profound human question of hope. The Hindu says, "Yes. We may hope for rescue beyond the flux of time." The naturalist might also say, "Yes. We hope through science and technology things will get better and better." This is a faith affirmation as much as the Hindu's belief in salvation outside of history. The existentialist might say, disillusioned with all faith-claims, "There is nothing to hope for at all. We must face a future of death with courage."

All of these options are grappling with the inescapable human question of our future, of what we might hope for. It is at this point that the Christian talk about eschatology comes in. At this level the Christian gospel competes with all other gospels which answer the question of what we might hope for. Christianity today stands or falls by whether its eschatology is the most profoundly responsive to the heights and lengths of human hope for a future which transcends the insuperable negativities of this present existence. Christians hope in the coming of the kingdom of God in and through history where all the negativities of existence are themselves negated; where tears will be wiped from our eyes, and there shall be an end to death, and to mourning and crying and pain, and all those who have died without fulfillment will be raised to perfection.

It is not enough to tell man to hope, for there is no health in sheer hoping. The sick man hopes to get well and the hungry man to have bread. After all, the dynamic of hope stems from the scope and the content of hope's vision. What are we to hope for; on what basis are we to hope? In whom are we to hope? John's apocalypse of the end of history is one of human fulfillment, of individual-personal, social-communal, and world-historical fulfillment. It is utterly staggering to the human imagination; it is fantastic. Most of us do not even believe it most of the time, even when as Christians and theologians we try to.

In going along with the major optimistic or pessimistic currents of our modern culture, we tend to believe that things are coming along all right, that we do not need to hope, that hope is after all a mirage, or that things are so bad, that ours is an age of such corruption and degradation, that even hope is too much to expect.

Harvey Cox became famous overnight writing most delightfully about the liberties and joys of "the secular city." His book is, as he calls it, a celebration of the liberties of the secular city and an invitation to its discipline. It is a wonderful book; the trouble is that there are no tears, no mourning, no crying, and no pain. It is hardly a book about the real world. The real world is more like a noisy chamber of cries arising from the agony of human beings who at this very time are dying under exploding bombs. Those who see the world as "the mature world which has come of age and which no longer needs God, because the world is really sufficient of itself" are disturbed by the question of God. The question of hope is really the question about God. Their problem is: since the world is getting along so well on its own, because of its empirical and pragmatic approach to life, it is hard to know at what point to introduce God. God seems so irrelevant in a world which has learned to solve its own problems or at least has an omnicompetent methodology. God is crowded out by the self-reliance of a tough-minded, problem-solving culture. It is hard to argue with that, but one can introduce other evidence and suggest another perspective. Quite another kind of testimony of our age says that God is impossible because of the tears and the suffering and the pain of life. The first group cannot put together man's affluence and God's presence — the new God-is-dead boys; the second group cannot hold together man's affliction and God's presence — the old God-is-dead boys.

The Christian gospel of hope puts together man's suffering and God's presence, and sees them as two sides of the same christological coin. The Christian gospel reveals the fate of the world from the hill of Golgotha, from the gas chambers built by Dachau's racial sadism, from Hiroshima's instant death and Vietnam's cruel realities. Albert Camus was one who loved love, but was driven to confess hopelessness in face of the impotence of love. He saw the story of Jesus as the sure proof of the powerlessness of love. But knowing nothing higher than human freedom and human love, he could glimpse no basis for a hope that stretches beyond the tears and the pain that accompany man to his death. He saw that ours is a time for radical love, for Christians and humanists and atheists to work together to decrease the number of murdered children, and to make man the center of love and freedom. But it is just the failure of love which unmasks the frailty of our hope.

Today, Christians must answer our age not only with our

love but also with our hope. Christians have love, Communists have hope — and hope is sometimes stronger than love. Others may love as well as we; and their love may fail as well as ours. But then what carries beyond the failure of love? It is only hope that can do that. Most Christians perhaps would say that the Christian message is basically and most deeply a message of love; the extent to which it is a promise of hope has not been so clear. This is a hope for a new heaven and a new earth, hope for the era when God will wipe away every tear from our eyes, and when there shall be an end to death and to mourning and crying and pain, and to poverty and discrimination and hatred and war. This is a hope which includes but also goes far beyond this or that improvement of the conditions of our society. It is hope for a new creation of absolute justice and absolute freedom.

Hope, Karl Jaspers says, must always be directed to the future. Christian hope is always directed to the future of God's unrestrained rule together with the liberation of creatures from their miseries. This is a future which pulls the Christian forward, a future of full life and full freedom and benevolent authority. The enemy of this future is death. The question is not merely whether Christians can love enough to share in the improvement of this life; that they can and should do. The question is also whether they can hope enough for the total renewal of the world, for a reconciliation of nature with nature, of man with nature, of man with man, of nation with nation, and of the whole world with God. Only if this hope is possible is it also possible to believe in God. Your picture of God is only as big as your hope.

Now there is no evidence from our world that we have a right to a great hope. Camus, I believe, went about as far as a humanist could go; he was an ardent activist, not a self-pitying fatalist. There is no evidence from our world either for the liberal faith in progress or for the Christian hope for a universal triumph over suffering and pain and death. Here is where we can only take God at his word, the word of his promise. We must press God hard, demanding that he stick to his promises. This promise is given most articulately in the resurrection of Jesus Christ. But what will that mean for us? We have only his promise and no other evidence that everything will come out all right in the end, that murdered children shall live, that the way of the righteous shall prosper, or that there will be an absolute end of death. We only have God's promise of a new creation. To equate this new creation with a secular metropolis is not so much a case of losing one's mind but rather of losing one's hope.

The faith that hangs on the promise of God gives birth to a hope that goes far beyond a concern for individual salvation. The future includes more than my future; my future cannot be separated from the all-inclusive future of mankind and from every living thing. We do not hope for ourselves alone and for only those who share our hope. We hope against hope for those who have no hope, and we hope for those whose hopes seem like illusions to us, or those whose hopes are shattered and unfilled. We hope for those who despair in life, even for those who destroy life.

The heart is so selfish that it tends to narrow the circle of hope and to divide mankind into halves, into the ins and outs. The universal hope of Christian faith which refuses to make ultimate distinctions between them and us is the source of the energy for taking the present seriously too. We have usually said that Christians are willing to get involved in the struggles of the world for decency and dignity, for freedom and life, by the push of faith active in love. May it not rather be by the pull of a hope that awaits and expects? I do not believe we would act unless we could hope; and I do not think we can hope unless there is real promise. As Christians we are to act as men with a hope. Perhaps what might restore to the church the power of mission is not more rhetoric about love, but the recovery of hope, a universal hope and an ultimate fulfillment of that promise of God which he made to us in good faith by raising Jesus from the dead.

Part Three

The Whole
Church

14

The
Future of the
Reformation

1 Cor. 13:13: "So faith, hope, love abide, these three; but the greatest of these is love."

William Hamilton, the theologian of "death-of-God" fame, has written in one of his more provocative articles, "Thursday's Child," that a generation can live on only one of these great lasting qualities at a time, faith or hope or love. The generation of the Reformation lived by faith. Today, he says, we cannot live by that faith; but we can live by hope. To us this is a great exaggeration, but it contains an element of truth. The great word of the Reformation was "faith." Not so much was said about love, and still less about hope. Faith was the focus, not faith as one among many other things, but "faith alone" became the battle cry of the Reformers. Faith alone counts in the vertical dimension; by faith alone can a man stand acceptable before God, and not by works. We are justified by grace through faith alone, with no chance of tipping the balance of God's judgment in our favor by the merits of our piety or morality.

All over the world we are celebrating the anniversary of the Reformation. The question has been raised, I am sure, in every planning committee, what is the appropriate thing to do in a new day of ecumenical ferment? For the past four hundred and fifty years we have been looking back to the

Reformation. *That* we have done so can hardly be blame-
worthy; but *how* we have done it has often been silly or
shameful. Have we not often acted like caretakers of a
cemetery, rather than watchmen on the towers? Has the Day
of the Reformation not been a day of eulogies? But eulogies
are appropriate only for the dead! Are we here today to
celebrate something dead, like the birthday of a great an-
cestor who died long ago? Or are we celebrating something
living with a still wonderful future? I am afraid that unwit-
tingly we have often in the past turned our Reformation Day
celebration into a sort of funeral service, and every sermon
into an obituary.

For the faith of the reformers we have often been satisfied
to substitute pride in the denominations which bear their
names. Martin Luther has been heroified as the George Washington of the Lutheran Church, and John Calvin the author
of the Constitution of the Divided States of Protestantism I
do not think we do well any longer to treat the Reformation
that way, not because we thereby claim too much for the
Reformation. Even in our pride we could not do that. But in
doing that we have been claiming too little. Lacking the
vitality of the faith which alone makes righteous, we have
opened the graves and examined the remains. We have
thought that by remembering the reformers with flowers on
their graves, and by reading with nostalgia the noble inscrip-
tions on their tombstones, and by singing the Reformation
Day rouser, "A Mighty Fortress," we were exhibiting the
same vitalities of faith as they had. We imagined that our task
was still to crusade against the tyrants of the Counter-
Reformation, long after they too had passed away. It may be,
in the sight of God, that a lot of our Reformation Day
rhetoric has been worse than the mischief of children on
halloween. Surely we must be ashamed of how many Protestant ministers have come out swinging with fists clenched
against the enemy and used the pulpit for their demagoguery
and to arouse bitter feelings and memories.

The faith of the Reformation is the faith worked alone by

God's grace, faith in Jesus Christ, faith which is anchored in the saving deeds of God in the history of redemption. But this faith does not stand alone. The fourth article of the Augsburg Confession is only one of the many. We are justified by an act of God alone, received through faith alone, and not by the works of our hands, by the thoughts in our heads, or by the feelings of our hearts. But this faith never stands alone. The sign of this faith is love. Love is the power to include those whom we naturally wish to exclude. This love does not draw a circle to keep me and mine inside, and to keep out thee and thine. It does not split humanity into us and them. The sign of this faith is a love that draws a circle around both thee and me, around both them and us. This love breaks down the walls of hostility; it dissipates the spirit of hatred; it drives toward the reunion of all those who are separated. This love is a celebration of what God has done to unite all mankind into the death and resurrection of his Son Jesus Christ. He came, he lived, he died for all, that all might be liberated through the power of his resurrection. The accompaniment of faith is love, a love that reaches out and clasps the hands of even the enemies of God. This faith which God works in the hearts of men is continually dwarfed and overshadowed by religious fanaticism, by intellectual pride, and a spirit of moralistic condemnation.

Somehow we Christians so often look more like the Pharisee than the publican, more like the elder son who stayed home than the prodigal, more like those who would pick up stones to throw at sinners than the one who reaches out to touch the hem of Jesus' garment, more like the high priests who sit in judgment than the lepers who call upon the name of Jesus for healing. And so we assume the mental complex of those who feel they are always in the right. The struggle about faith dealt with this sort of thing in the sixteenth century. Faith frees us from religious self-preoccupation.

To use the words of Søren Kierkegaard, faith, justifying faith, generates the edifying thought that before God we are always in the wrong, and therefore we never have to prove we are in the right. This is a faith which is right and makes right because it grasps the righteousness of God in Christ, and does not seek after human credits and merit badges as things to flaunt in the face of God and to boast about in the face of man. It is a faith which is so busy doing good that it forgets to worry about the question of being good.

This faith, as we have said, is never alone. It generates love. There are those who say we have finally broken through to the epoch of love. If a generation can live on only one at a time, either faith or hope or love, surely it must be love on which we thrive today, love which marks the genius of our times. Are we not living in an ecumenical age? Isn't ours an age of ecumenical dialogue? Certainly, we have come a long way in breaking down barriers to understanding, in merging our efforts in common associations like the World Council of Churches, as well as national and city councils of churches. The Second Vatican Council was summoned by a Pope whose charity toward other Christians was overflowing. Small groups of Christians are uniting, and where there is not church union, there may be common worship and prayer in a spirit of love. We have felt the breezes of love that are driven by faith, and they are refreshing.

There are those in our churches, however, who read the ecumenical age as a betrayal of the Protestant heritage, who see the World Council of Churches as a Communist conspiracy, and who harden their hearts against the love that is driven by faith. The truth of the matter, however, is quite the opposite. For love that is driven by faith, by the real faith of the reformers, arouses hope. Hope does not turn our heads backward, but toward the future. A genuine faith is anchored in the past. From it there springs forth love that is restlessly active in the present, and both together create a hope that dreams of a future that transcends infinitely the limitations in the church and in the world of the present age — an absolute future that rescues us from the tyrannies of the past and the status quo.

The danger to the ecumenical movement today is that it

will settle for a posture of dialogue, that it will say, "so far and no farther." The danger is not that we will return to an age of fanatical faith that thrives on open hatred and religious wars. The threat is rather that we will have come so far from the period of hot wars, only to land in an ecumenical stalemate of a thwarted love that expresses itself in tolerance of mere dialogue, of friendly conversations across the fences that still divide us. But unending dialogue across the barriers that stand between the churches means an eternal breach in the unity of Christians, in the body of which Christ is the sole head. Our temptation is to allow the ecumenical movement to become a new and subtle phase of a cold war between churches, friendly, civil, and tolerant on the surface, no doubt, but stubborn and turgid in the depths of our minds. Conservatives today may be afraid of even dialogue, but many liberals hide a secret fear of anything that goes beyond dialogue toward the reunion of all of us who were split apart during the Reformation.

The faith of the Reformation cannot stand alone, content to see its devotees permanently transfixed in bondage to the bitter feelings stirred by the hot and cold wars of our religious traditions. This faith is active in love, and this love must live by the hope of reunion, or else faith becomes fanatical and love becomes anemic. A true love cannot accept dialogue as a permanent fate, for dialogue is only the best that love can do among those who are still separated. But hope pulls love forward into a brand new future which beckons us beyond dialogue. If love does not drive us toward reunion, it becomes changed into sentimentality.

We need to be challenged to make way for a new birth of hope, springing from faith in the absolute future. This vision of our coming God in the power of his kingdom transcends the paltry dreams of a faltering faith and a flickering love. Our faith is in a God of hope, the God of the absolute future. We do not, therefore, hope for a repetition of the last four hundred and fifty years. We hope for a future which will witness the victory of the Reformation faith, a future of fulfillment of faith, not as we have dreamed of conquest, at the expense of the well-being of others, but a victory of faith in mutual fulfillment in the communion of love. The victory of faith is the triumph of the kingdom of God in history, expressing its power through peace in the church, unity among the people of God, justice for all mankind, and a mission of redemption and hope to the world that groans in a universal travail for emancipation.

The future of the Reformation is not the future of something called Protestantism, but the future of faith, fulfilled in love and hope in a reunited church of Jesus Christ on earth. All this for the sake of the universal health and wholeness and happiness of all mankind.

We will enter into the next four hundred and fifty years in the hope by which we are saved. Without hope neither love nor faith can thrive or survive. The sixteenth-century Reformation was blunted very quickly because the rediscovery of the gospel of faith was confined to the churches as a point of confessional controversy or mired down into the inner recesses of subjective piety among individual believers. That faith did not release sufficiently the dynamic of love among Christians and between churches, and a stunted love could not yield a great harvest of hope for a magnificent future which God has planned for us. So in the last four hundred and fifty years we have received about as much as we have hoped. But our hopes have been measly and miserly.

The next four hundred and fifty years will begin to tell the story whether Christians and churches remain enclosed within themselves, or whether they turn to the world with the gospel of hope. If they turn to the world buoyed up by the power and promise of hope, if their concern is for the whole world, then the reunion of the churches will happen in the course of time. The unity of the church will be God's gift to an obedient church, as God's eschatological mission in history is carried out. The reunion of the churches cannot happen by the wizardry of lawyers who write new constitutions for hybrid organizations. That seems to be the usual

Protestant strategy toward unity. It will happen in the course of the churches being pulled by the future of God into a suffering world, that is, into a world whose future at this time hangs precariously in the balance.

It may very well be that God is withholding unity from the church until she regains her sense of mission in an age of universal history. For Christians to hope for unity without undertaking the obligation of mission to the world would be to enjoy privilege without responsibility. A church that is not hoping for the redemption of the world has plenty of time for ecclesiastical bickering and sniping. When soldiers are back in the barracks with time on their hands, they fight and quarrel. When they are in the foxholes, they are buddies who help each other, even to the last drop of blood.

If in realism we turn to the past, we will express gratitude to God for the faith of our fathers. On this Reformation Day we do thank God that the faith of Paul and Peter and John, of all the apostles and the whole catholic church in history, has been handed down to us through Luther and all the reformers in our traditions, who under the Spirit of Christ have kept the memories of faith alive and burning, so that we too could believe. Even so we do not want a repetition of the miseries of the past. We are able to endure the present and look to the future as a brand new stretch of God's time because we live by hope. Hope means waiting for something we do not yet possess. We do not have any guarantees. We live in hope toward the future which we cannot see. It is God's future for the world. If we could not have this hope for the world as we face the future, we would exist in a state of unrelieved pain and tension. For the church we see within us and around us gives us little ground for hope; and the world we see is a place of tears. The men around us and those who lead us show very little evidence that they have "come of age." Still we hope for the future. We do not believe that the next four hundred and fifty years need to be a boring and grim repetition of the follies of men in the past. For the God of history is the God of hope, the Lord of the future.

Our hope is not based on illusions; it is not the painting of pictures with the brush of wishful thinking; it is not filling a utopia with the substance of human optimism. Our hope is an uncanny hope. God revealed that this hope can stand in spite of Hiroshima and Vietnam. As St. Paul said, "This hope is that in the end the whole of created life will be rescued." This is the message of "hope against hope." The message of the Reformation will seek fulfillment today through us, as we seek to build up new hopes in mankind, anchored in the power of God's future.

15

Three Sure
Ways to Make
a Sect

My text is from the Augsburg Confession, the little
bible of the Reformation. "For the true unity of the
church it is enough to agree concerning the teaching
of the Gospel and the administration of the sacraments" (Art. VII).

INTRODUCTION

According to our usual Reformation Day mythology,
Luther pulled the church out of the Dark Ages. That myth
has lost a lot of its luster. For one thing, the ages were not so
dark as we thought and, for another, they were not followed
by so much enlightenment as we believed. More important
still, realities of our day have broken through to tell us the
church is still in dark ages. Even after a decade of ecumenical
hope, hope in spite of our fractured histories, we do not see
much light at the other end of the tunnel.

If we look at the churches as they actually are, we see few
trends that betoken an early fulfillment of our ecumenical
vision. Our greatest need now is to take a new look beyond
ecumenism, to find out where we are, where we ought to be.
We need a sober diagnosis. Just a few years ago we heard
brave words about man having come of age, about the church
coming out of its adolescence, and theology demythologizing
its way to maturity. That sounds pretty silly now. We are still
in the dark ages; and so the reformation must go on.

Ecclesia semper reformanda. That's a slogan we are used to hearing; it's supposed to be our speciality. But it is too great and important a task to leave to Lutherans. Welcome on board, all who believe the gospel of Jesus Christ and who live toward the kingdom that established the church in his name – Catholics from every nation and Protestants from any denomination.

For a long time Reformation Day was celebrated as the story of Martin Luther. The slogan was "back to Luther." Then Lutherans became historically more sophisticated with the advent of the Luther-renaissance. That was an exciting time of new discovery, from Karl Holl to Joseph Lortz. So we placed our celebrations under the banner of "forward to Luther," to use the phrase coined by Anders Nygren. But, of course, that is literally an historical impossibility. That would have to presuppose we're still in the Middle Ages. The Luther-event is an historical fact; as such it can never happen again. If we go back we find only the records, the shrines and fossils of past history. If we go forward, we can never have a repristination of something in our past. That is just the way it is to live in history.

So what is this day, this celebration, all about? It's not a case of going back; it's not a case of turning back the clock; it's not a case of projecting our past into the future; it's not a case of visiting a museum housing our favorite mummy. Rather, it is a matter of joining ourselves to the unfinished struggle for the gospel and to join the movement of the Word in history. The struggle for the gospel – that's what the Luther-event means in world history. We are being asked whether we know what the struggle is all about today, whether we know where to plant the dynamite of the gospel in the rotting structures of a church that still lives in the dark ages.

Our point of departure is the same as Luther's – a deepening conviction that darkness has come upon the church. It is a mark of the secular world to claim to be enlightened, to imagine it lives under the bright light of reason and progress. It is a mark of the church to let the light of the gospel shine

into its darkness, the only light that darkness cannot overcome. Where the gospel is, never fear, there is the church.
The whole ecumenical movement is now stumbling on the
rocks, because too many forces within it believed you could
reverse the proposition, that is, "Where the church is, there is
the gospel." Luther's struggle was for the gospel, and therefore also for the church. But for the sake of the purity of the
gospel, he was even willing to blow the unity of the institutional church. That is hard for an ecumenical age to grasp.

Wherever we go we find some degree of awareness that our
best ecumenical formulae are not working out. Like Humpty
Dumpty, we are discovering in the church that all the king's
horses and all the king's men couldn't put Humpty Dumpty
together again.

It is indeed painful for us to say that we are at the end of
the ecumenical era, that the "coming great church" that leading ecumenists prophesied a decade ago is just not coming
along. The "new reformation," as it was called, was to be the
triumphal procession of a reunited Christendom into the
post-modern world. Today we are paying the price for such
blasphemy. We are heading toward a new age of sectarianism.
A sect comes about by pursuing a sectarian treatment of the
gospel. There are three sure ways to make a sect. A sect
happens when the gospel of the church undergoes a distor-
tion, a reduction. In the light of the gospel, there were three
ways to make a sect in Luther's day. They are the perennial
ways; so they can be seen today too.

1. THE REDUCTION TO THE CHURCH

All we need for the unity of the church is the gospel. That
is what Art. VII of the Augsburg Confession says. This is the
gospel of the kingdom of God and of his righteousness that
has arrived in Jesus Christ, and that has created the church as
an instrument and as a sacrament of the gospel for the sake
of the whole world. Three terms — the kingdom of God, the
church, and the world — suggest the three ways to make a
sect. Three poles: reduce the gospel to one of them and you

have got a beautiful sect. Let's take first the church. That is where it all began. The reduction of the gospel to the church means the church has become its own Lord, by building institutionally and dogmatically the guarantee of its own identity into itself. A fancy term for this is ecclesiocentricity. We commonly speak of egocentricity. An egocentric person in intolerable unless he is trying to be funny. But the church in Luther's day was not trying to be comical. It controlled the means and the destinies of the souls of men. The Roman party was sectarian, because it cramped the catholicity of the church into an Italian mold.

This reduction of the gospel to the church happens in our day too. Its most common form is bureaucratic Christianity. The church runs by self-studies and future planning, keeping the little wheels spinning around the big wheels. It happens too when the church lives at the expense of the world, when she acts as though the kingdom will come by more people joining the church, when she uses the world as a stepping stone to a higher throne among the powers of this world. This muscular picture of the church is a hangover from her sectarian past. The struggle for the gospel is waged against this puffed-up church, the church of the grand inquisitor, the church of power and worldly wealth. It is a struggle for the humility of the church, for the poverty of the church, for a penitent church of pilgrim people. So Luther said, how come Christ traveled on foot, but the Pope travels in a palanquin with a retinue of three or four thousand mule drivers; how come Christ washed the feet of sinners but the Pope has them kiss his toes?

2. THE REDUCTION OF THE GOSPEL TO THE WORLD

The second sure way to make a sect, in Luther's day and ours, is to reduce the gospel to a secular humanism, to cut it down to the size of the world's enlightenment. Luther at times feared that Erasmus of Rotterdam, the leading humanist luminary of his day, was afflicted by a greater misunderstanding of the gospel than his Roman opponents. Luther would heat things up; Erasmus kept things cool, never going beyond room temperature. But Luther felt the humanistic embrace could be the kiss of death.

The church in the modern world was the dominant theme of the Second Vatican Council. Sometimes it has seemed since as though there is a tug of war going on between two types of sectarians, the conservatives, the restorationists, who want to cling to the past, who stick to the Latin forms in church organization, cult, and doctrine, and on the other side the secularizers, who are so exhilarated by the modern world that they become imitators of every doctrine and fad, not taking their time to make everything captive to Christ. These modernists are just as sectarian as the Curia conservatives, who have their heads screwed on backward.

This same deadly polarity exists in all our churches. The battle between biblical fundamentalists and the modernists who take their norms from a modern *ism*, from some cult or ideology, is a case of two types of sects fighting each other. To disclose their sectarian nature, it was necessary for Luther to offend both the Romanists and the humanists by using the little word *sola*. It was *sola gratia*, by grace alone, it was *sola fide*, by faith alone, it was *solus Christus*, Christ alone. The purpose of the word *alone* was to reveal the sectarian character of those who make the gospel captive to the church or to the modern world.

Secular Christianity is a dis-grace; literally it wants to go it alone without grace. The Christian is asked to be just a good secular man, celebrating the world come of age, and the church strikes the silly pose of drooling at the world, a world which has allegedly found its way to the broad daylight of scientific thinking and technological efficiency — the very means of salvation that can turn upon us and kill us all — first our souls, then our bodies!

3. THE REDUCTION OF THE GOSPEL TO A FUTURE KINGDOM

There is a third way to make a sect. The secular version of this is revolutionary utopianism, where the children of today are slaughtered on the altar of tomorrow, where men worship the Moloch of the future, making burned offerings today in the form of bullets and bombings. Luther had to struggle on this front too. There was a group of religious enthusiasts, who had a lot going for them. They looked for a radical kingdom of the poor, the peasantry, the proletariat of that time. Surely we are not saying Luther was right in calling upon the princes to slaughter the peasants. But we are saying that, whatever the right or wrong on that particular question, the struggle for the gospel was still involved. Is the gospel an enthusiasm that gives a person wings to leave the present? The gospel does not take sides with the future against the present; it does not call us to forget this world and join the future.

Since the Reformation, Christianity has spawned scores of tiny eschatological sects, whose lot in life was so miserable, all they could think about was jumping into the clouds and going to heaven, getting themselves translated into another world. The gospel is not about a kingdom of the future, which makes us write off this world as a hopeless cause; it is rather about the future of the kingdom that presses itself into history, in the person of Christ and in those incorporated into his love, his freedom, his peace, and the fullness of his life. It is the future of Christ that is really present where the living Word is preached and the sacraments are administered, as signs of the New Reality that the world also is created to enjoy. Christ is not our private thing; the gospel is not our personal philosophy. The gospel of Christ is the forward thrust of the kingdom of God that arrives with power to justify the world, to make it righteous, to bring it home to its happier future in God. The eschatological enthusiasts did not use the power of the future to care for this world, but instead as an excuse to ignore it, or just blast it to hell.

CONCLUSION

Thus we have three reductions of the gospel, three sure ways to make a sect — leading to ecclesiocentricity (church-centered thinking), secular humanism (man-centered thinking), and enthusiasm (utopian or otherworldly futurism). These are marks of sectarianism in Christianity today, visible here and there in the youth movement, in the conservative backlash, in the "God-is-dead" theologies, just to cite a few examples.

The tragedy of our dilemma is that the struggle for the gospel which was taken up to combat sectarian treatments of the gospel itself ended up producing a sect. This sect of the gospel became established, called itself a church, and then others named it the Lutheran Church. In a kind of self-forgetfulness we have adopted the name of our opponents, and call ourselves Lutherans. So here we are, wondering who we are. However, the world does not need any of our sectarian denominations. It needs a new movement of the gospel of Jesus Christ. It needs the peace and laughter of the kingdom of God; it needs the righteousness and love that became intense in the cross of Jesus; it needs the wholeness and fullness that flow from the glory of God, arousing wonder and ecstasy in the hearts of men. The good news of the revolution of the kingdom in Jesus is creating a movement of new vitalities coursing through the varicose veins of a church with tired blood. That is where the action is, getting into the movement of that gospel. Where the gospel of Jesus Christ is preached, there is the church; our sectarianisms can fade away, giving rise to a new and better day.

16

Be a
Pluralist
for Christ's
Sake!

1 Cor. 3:21-23: "For all things are yours, whether
Paul or Apollos or Cephas or the world or life or
death or the present or the future, all are yours; and
you are Christ's; and Christ is God's."

Here is a fantastic thought, that everything is yours, that
you do not have to split up reality and take only part of it,
that you do not have to divide the world and live within a
half of it, that you can be open to all the good of the present
and of the future, and to the insights of Paul and Peter and
James and John. You can be a pluralist for Christ's sake. All
things are yours, because you are Christ's and Christ is God's,
and he shall be all in all. That is a fantastic vision. It is not a
boring unity and a static uniformity. It is a rich variety, a
dynamic pluriformity.

Pluralism is both a problem and a promise. Consider first
the problem. Dietrich Bonhoeffer visited America in 1939.
When he returned to Germany, he wrote an article called,
"Protestantism without a Reformation." He lamented the
fact that it has been granted to the Americans less than any
other nation on earth to realize the visible unity of the
church of God. Of course he was right. Nowhere and never in
two thousand years has there existed so many varieties of

Christianity as in America, so many churches and denominations and synods and sects with so many creeds and cults and styles of life. The church unity movement came to America about twenty-five years ago, and since then we have been on a mad rush to unity. The unity of the church has been proclaimed, and we have felt guilty for not manifesting it. Our pluralism was a problem because it was getting in the way of unity. Formulae were created to bring about mergers and church unions. The most colossal attempt is still in the making, the so-called COCU — the Consultation on Church Union. It goes back to the Blake-Pike proposal, offering a quite obvious formula. If you take evangelical and episcopal and reformed and catholic traditions together, you can make one great church body out of Methodists and Episcopalians and Presbyterians and Disciples and Brethren and lots of others. So it looks like at least some Protestants are doing something about pluralism as a problem. There are those who feel that there is no reason why so comprehensive a formula could not make room for Baptists and Lutherans, if not also Roman Catholics and Eastern Orthodox.

I happen to be a Lutheran of sorts, and therefore among the holdouts — we are not a part of COCU — so it may appear in poor taste to raise the slightest doubt about this great formula of church union. But I must confess that I am not enthusiastic about it, and I am not knocking myself out trying to convince Lutherans to join it. There are Lutherans, of course, who want to be included in everything, so they feel spasms of guilt for not being along with the latest wave of the future. Perhaps, as Lutherans, we could add another ingredient — namely, pure doctrine — sound Lutheran theology. There are those who say that COCU is lacking some of that. The little they have comes from the old Evangelical and Reformed Church. But I do not believe this is a genuine way to handle the problem of pluralism; I do not believe it holds much promise for the future. Like the remarriage of grandmother, one doesn't expect much in the way of offspring. Or, if you don't like the metaphor, for gramma's sake, you may think of it as an overly ripe fruit of the ecumenical ethos that is now passed. You know what overly ripe fruit is like: it is soft and mushy, and not very good for eating.

The problem is that we do not yet have an answer to the problem of the pluralism that works among us as a source of division. We do not yet have a model of structural unity that could embrace the different histories of Eastern and Western Christianity, of Roman and Reformation Christianity, of the younger churches in the Third World and the mother churches from the colonial nations.

What can we do about a problem we cannot solve? We may flip it over and see it as a promise. We may actually see pluralism as a promise. We may discover a new shape of unity when we overcome our contempt for pluralism, when we free the gospel from its bondage to monolithic images and uniform structures, to homogeneous ideals and doctrines which are quick to foster schisms and sects, heresies and anathemas.

The church is bound to be pluralistic, for all things are pure, not only the things of a sacred past, but also the things of a secular present and an unknown future. The church is open to new things that happen on the frontline of history. Pluralism is of the essence of a church that functions on the borderline of the new and the old, of a church that is open in all directions, toward the world, toward the present, and toward the future, as Paul says. It is the reality of the kingdom of God that places the church in a pioneering role, driving the church to integrate the abundant forms of life in the world into the future of God's kingdom.

The pluralism of the church is a promise when it comes about by affirming many forms and styles of spiritual and social life. She affirms various conditions of life that have to do with sex and age and tribe and language and race and culture and nationality. Just this openness to the world in its fantastic variety is the statement of the gospel: "All things are yours, whether bearing the stamp of the apostles like Paul or Peter, or whether of the world in its present and future."

The church is pluralistic when, in openness to the world

and its future, she does not shun new styles and new methods, new ideas and new conditions of experience and learning. She does not live and breathe only in a sacred atmosphere, confining herself to a sacred style and a sacred theology, a sacred language and a sacred music. The church's pluralism keeps her open also to things sanctioned and hallowed by the past, but this will not make her sneer at the new styles that seem religiously empty and profane.

The world is mixed with evil. Paul also warned against being conformed to the world, of becoming slaves to the elemental spirits of the universe, of being made a prey by philosophy and empty deceits. These warnings were not given to make the church nervous, to scare it off from trying new things. The church has had to take the risk of being the church in the world, of baptizing all kinds of things in the name of Christ. For all things belong to Christ. It doesn't matter who made it or where it comes from; if it is real, it is ours. There is nothing — there is no place and no time — off limits to us, because we are Christ's. Nothing in nature, nothing in history, nothing in the country, nothing in the city, nothing in the past, nothing in the future! This is a risky kind of universalism. We are often taught to look down our nose at medieval Christianity, as though it were all a dark tunnel of centuries from Augustine to Luther. But it excelled in something genuinely of the gospel, symbolized in the great medieval cathedrals and in the great scholastic systems. They were saying in the concrete, all things are ours, everything from the gargoyles to the angels; that's all ours, because we are Christ's and Christ is God's. It is a catholic vision.

This is never an achievement that we can tuck away into a sacred past. The church is still on the way to achieve true catholicity, to bring everything present and future into captivity to Christ, to reclaim everything real for the domain of God's kingdom.

Hence, the pluralism that is a problem, when the church looks to itself and wonders how it can make one reality out of so many differences, may become a promise when it is seen as a mark of the church's openness to the world and its myriad forms of life. When the church is on her missionary way, true to her calling to go to the ends of the world until the end of time, she will bring the witness of the gospel that all things are good. They are here to be enjoyed, for Christ has been given a throne in the midst of reality, and has redeemed it for its fullness in the life of God.

17

Reformation
Means
Freedom

My text is a mosaic of sayings that ring out whenever we think of the Reformation. The first is what Luther said: "A Christian man is a perfectly free lord of all, subject to no one. A Christian man is a perfectly dutiful servant of all, subject to everyone." Luther came along fifteen hundred years too late for that to be included in the canon. But there are a few others like it, and Luther had them in mind. "The righteous shall live by faith, and not by the works of the law." That is, he pits faith and freedom against law and order. Paul said, "Although I am free, I make myself the servant of all." Jesus said, "You shall know the truth and the truth shall make you free . . . . If the Son makes you free, you are free indeed."

We are gathered together because the Reformation happened, and we have not yet forgotten it. Every year, at least once a year, we do our thing: we hear a sermon about the Reformation and its hero, Luther. In many quarters the enthusiasm for this day has waned. Ours is an ecumenical age; the old insults against Roman Catholics which nourished so much of the excitement of the day have lost their charm. Besides that, many people are hard put to state just what we moderns do have in common with the Reformation anyway. What are we celebrating? Do we still share Luther's faith and vision? Is it not the case that for years what brought Protes-

tants together was not something they were all for, but rather
something they were all against — Catholics. The sociologists'
definition of a Protestant in America is that he's not a Jew or
a Catholic.

If we take an honest look at Luther and the Reformation
we must admit that we see a very strange and ambiguous
phenomenon, strange, I say, because from where we stand as
modern men, the Reformation looks more like the last part
of the Middle Ages than of a piece with our modern period;
and ambiguous, I say, because the Reformation brought more
problems than solutions. It triggered off a series of historical
events that have had catastrophic results, reaching down to
our own time. No celebration of the Reformation can be
honest, without acknowledging that the Reformation was for
the most part quite in line with the Middle Ages, and without
acknowledging that it brought about much suffering, oppression, and still unresolved difficulties both in the church and in
the world. (I admit that we are seemingly off to a poor start,
moodwise, for a big celebration, but I believe if we work
through these ideas, we will be free to celebrate what the
Reformation is good for, free to celebrate on the road to
freedom that Luther paved through faith in the gospel of
Jesus Christ.) Freedom is the heart of the Reformation; freedom is the unfinished business of the gospel in the world
today. We are linked with the Reformation through the cause
of freedom which the gospel poses as our common future.
But before we can joyfully acclaim our alliance with the Reformation's revolution for freedom, we must backtrack to
what we said about the strangeness and the ambiguity of
the Reformation.

1. THE STRANGENESS OF THE REFORMATION
    If we happen to be Protestants or otherwise think of our-
selves as lucky heirs of the Reformation, we must account for
the fact that most other people cannnot see what we have to
boast about. Is it not true that even we as theologians have
given the impression that Luther is a modern man, full of

relevant ideas for the modern world? Is it not true that we have acted as though there is nothing wrong with us that a big dose of Luther and the Reformation could not cure? Is it not so that we have kept on telling ourselves to be true to the Reformation, as though *its* norms and ideas could simply function in our day in the same way? We have wanted to downplay that Luther was also a child of the Middle Ages.

A few years ago Lutherans from around the world struggled in Helsinki to bring the doctrine of justification up to date. That is supposed to be the Lutheran specialty. What happened was that Luther's answers were not fitting the modern questions in a direct way. There were few who realized why. What was forgotten was that Luther's message of justification by faith alone without the works of the law was very liberating for Luther because he lived under the oppressive system of penances. A man's salvation was really dependent on a kind of ecclesiastical sweepstakes, in which the individual was gambling for salvation with all he had earned by his works. The system was calculated to keep him betting and guessing, and Luther could never be sure of where he was. But now we do not live within the same kind of priestly and sacramental system of control, which metes out salvation by degrees, subject to a legalistic calculus of good works.

Secondly, Luther attacked the authority of the Pope and the ecclesiastical office, but he exchanged that for a view about the authority of Scripture which has become increasingly more problematic even in the churches that bear his name. The history of Protestantism is full of disputes about the nature and scope of biblical authority. Luther posed the authority of the Bible against the authority of the papal office, but in doing that he did what many other medieval men before him had done. The Roman Catholics have had their problem with papal authority. But, let us face it, Protestants have scarcely been better off; the present-day squabbles about hermeneutics are proof of that. When Protestants say, the Bible is the authority, they are not able to answer,

"Whose interpretation of the Bible?" In any case, our modern problems are not the same as Luther's. Our concept of the nature of authority in human life has changed. As modern men, we do not accept at face value any authorities imposed from above. We will not sacrifice our own personal judgment based on personal knowledge and experience to any outside authority. No word that is felt to violate the structures of reason and experience is acceptable. Needless to say, modern men, even modern men who happen to be Christians, have not settled the question of authority in its relation to freedom. If we in the churches of the Reformation had an answer to that question that could even satisfy ourselves, we would be extremely fortunate.

Thirdly, all through the Middle Ages the idea prevailed that the unity of the church depended on complete agreement over doctrine. In that respect Luther was no different from the theologians of the Roman Church. Luther and his followers demanded uniformity of doctrine as the basis of church unity, and those who did not conform were persecuted and driven out. Fierce religious wars were fought. There was no room for pluralism, no toleration of differences, no concept of religious liberty as that which we are allowed to enjoy.

Luther wanted to reform the church and to base the unity of the church on the correct and pure doctrine of the Gospel. Lutherans today sometimes pay lip service to the ideal of pure doctrine, but in practice the Lutheran churches, like all other modern churches, including the Roman Church, tolerate vast differences of doctrine. As a matter of fact, most of us enjoy a healthy amount of *pluralism* in the same church, in the same school, even in the same family. We have come a long, long way from the medieval assumptions on which Luther launched his reformation. I hope we can be candid enough to acknowledge that our hero to a great extent stands in the mold of the Middle Ages, and shares in what seems to us its remoteness and strangeness from modern times.

2. AMBIGUITY OF THE REFORMATION

We cannot merely view the Reformation as the tail-end of the Middle Ages. It is also the start of something new. We cannot look at the Reformation in and of itself; we cannot understand the Reformation except by looking at its fruits. Here is where Catholics have had trouble figuring out what we had to cheer about on Reformation Day. Look at the unforeseen and unwanted results of Luther's achievement. Luther wanted to reform the entire church, but instead the church broke up into many little pieces. Every attempt to restore the unity has been in vain. Yet it is precisely this destruction of the unity of the church that forms a root cause of most of modern history. The loss of church unity promoted and hastened the rise of the secular states and our secular culture. The secularizing of the state, the disestablishment of religion, was a direct result of the bloody religious wars in which millions of Catholics and Lutherans and other Protestants were killing each other off. Each of the religious parties was fighting to make its concept of Christian truth binding on the entire nation or territory. For the sake of sheer survival the states had to secularize themselves, to push religion away from the center of things to the periphery, to get rid of religion so far as it had been the basis of political unity.

Because Christianity had blood on its hands, because Christian leaders had become murderers in their zeal for the truth, the faith itself was disgraced. Religion had to be handcuffed and confined to the prison sphere of the private personal life of each individual. Churches became associations for people to share their religious feelings and beliefs, but religion had to retreat from the public sphere. We are still suffering from this hangover, whenever we hear that the church ought to stay out of politics, and pastors ought to stick to religious subjects and not go putting their nose into social and public matters like Rev. Groppi and the Berrigan brothers, or not speak out on Vietnam, ABM, welfare reform, the military-industrial complex, and Watergate.

Without the Reformation, there would have been no splitting of the church; with no splitting of the church, there
would have been no religious wars; with no religious wars, no
need to secularize the state and the general culture, to
remove religion from the public to the private sphere. Since
religion has been confined to the inner-life, or is made a mere
matter of the after-life, it has been charged with irrelevance.
The church is being criticized as just not engaged with the
serious human issues of our time. Thus, when we celebrate
the Reformation, we cannot do it in good conscience without
confessing that it brought forth many trends and tendencies
which are extremely ambiguous, and not all to the good.

3. REFORMATION: ROAD TO FREEDOM

Finally, I want to confess that in spite of the strangeness
and ambiguity of the Reformation, and of Luther, its chief
leader, there is something there that we may dearly love —
something that was born or reborn which makes the Reformation an unforgettable landmark in that history of freedom worked by faith. The permanent significance of the
Reformation is assured wherever men study the story of
freedom and seek to add a new chapter to that history by
pioneering a new freedom movement, proclaiming liberty to
the captives, and paving the rocky road to freedom.

Luther preached and experienced the freedom of the
Christian man, because faith was an immediate personal relation, an inner participation in the truth and reality of God.
Out of this faith grew the freedom of criticism. He could
criticize the very means that made this faith possible in the
first place. He could criticize the Bible, the church, and all its
offices and institutions. He could criticize any human authority, especially when we are tempted to put too much reliance
on it. The seeds of freedom were planted by this faith in
God. A man is free from every alien law; he can write new
laws out of his new relation to God. He is subject to no law
and to no Lord, but he himself is the lord of all, mature
enough to rule himself. But this freedom is not just a formal

freedom of an isolated man clamoring about his rights. It is a freedom founded on truth, and it exhibits itself in caring for other people. This freedom makes the Christian a servant of all, subject to the demands of love for everyone.

Out of this faith in God that gives birth to freedom, we cannot be satisfied to go on the pilgrimage of freedom only as far as Luther went. The road to freedom leads on to the future where no man has walked. We must carry the burdens for freedom in the present for those who have collapsed or have been laid up on the way. We must widen the road to freedom, so that all our brothers and sisters can find it, and together walk on a highway that takes us to the homeland of our future in God. Our task on this road is that of unburdening everyone who is stumbling alone, to help a man to his feet, to help those who stray get back on the track, to encourage those who stop in their tracks, thinking that we have gone far enough on the road to freedom, that we ought to settle down now and try to build an abiding city. As heirs of the Reformation, we must widen the range of freedom way beyond anything Luther attempted. He did not meet the full challenge of freedom. While he had a good grasp of the freedom of the Christian man, made possible by faith in Christ, he did not carry the fight for freedom fully into the political realm. There he stopped short with a kind of "law and order" mentality, and called for obedience to the ruling orders and authorities.

He was no great champion for the freedom of the citizen and the human rights that we now take for granted in our constitutional democracies. Let us not pretend that Lutherans were ever at the forefront of this struggle for freedom in the political order. Others were carrying our burdens and blazing the trail for our freedoms. Let us not forget to thank God this day for the heroic deeds of left-wing Protestants and humanists, who usually are given the short end on Reformation Day.

And let us not forget those who have carried the struggle for freedom into the economic field, for the social revolutionaries who first dreamed of freedom for all people from economic slavery, and even laid their lives on the line in liberating children, women, and workers from the miseries of overwork, long hours, lousy pay, and inhumane working conditions.

The freedom movement must be carried into all fields today. We must open up new fronts; when it seems the battle has been won on one front, we must move ahead to spy on new forms of liberty, and not only in terms of the external conditions of life. We need not only more freedom for more people, but deeper freedom for each person. What good does it do if the whole world becomes free, if we eliminate the causes of political, social, and economic slavery, only to find that we are slaves to inner drives and desires, that we are hooked on hangups which make us enemies of ourselves?

The road to freedom has not come to an end. We can celebrate the Reformation and the role of Luther and Calvin and Zwingli and their lesser lieutenants, because they were on the road to freedom, and because they erected some signposts which we can follow, which point ahead to the ultimate future of freedom to which our faith in Jesus Christ is leading us. If we see the Reformation as a station along the road to freedom, then what I said about its strangeness and its ambiguous effects in history does not deprive us of the joy of this day, of celebrating the realities of freedom which we share with the reformers through the one and the same faith in the truth of God's love and the grace he has brought in Christ.

18

Ecumenism: Where Do We Go From Here?

John 17:20-26: "I do not pray for these only, but also for those who believe in me through their word, that they may all be one; even as thou, Father, are in me, and I in thee, that they also may be in us, so that the world may believe that thou hast sent me. The glory which thou has given me I have given them, that they may be one even as we are one, I in them and thou in me, that they may become perfectly one, so that the world may know that thou has sent me and has loved them even as thou hast loved me. Father, I desire that they also, whom thou hast given me, may be with me where I am, to behold my glory which thou hast given me in thy love for me before the foundation of the world. O righteous Father, the world has not known thee, but I have known thee; and these know that thou hast sent me. I made known to them thy name, and I will make it known, that the love with which thou hast loved me may be in them, and I in them."

What are the prospects of ecumenism in America? Churches have come out of their isolation. They have gone through a period of extended courtship; some have even dared to get engaged. But we have to concede at this time, the prospects of marriage are not very bright. The path of ecumenism has moved from conversation to collaboration, and to the very brink of consolidation. But it is at this point that the ecumenical train seems to be grinding to a stop. People are pulling back from the prospects of one huge agglomeration of churches in a pan-Protestant union. Many people are not sure that the ecumenical plans of the 1960s should be consummated in the seventies. This is not to belittle the authentic ecumenical experiences of the sixties. The adventure of seeking and finding long lost brothers and sisters of the faith was exciting and needs no defense. But we extrapolated from that experience to imagine that soon there would be a family reunion, perhaps under one church structure. So the ecumenical movement became institutionalized. We set up offices to send out the invitations, to plan the homecoming events, and to make the prospects of life together in a reunited church most appealing to everyone.

Now it seems that the dream has burst like a soap bubble. Some are saying ecumenism is dead. Especially young people are uninspired by this bureaucratic ecumenism that creeps along through proper channels and offices. In the 1960s the idea of a pan-Protestant union of churches in America had a certain magic ring. Today the project arouses about as much passion as would a proposal to merge the International and the Continental Can Companies. Ecumenism was once the bold journey of the avant-garde in the churches. Today it is a file folder in a cabinet at church headquarters. If ecumenism is not dead, at least it seems to have come under the deadening control of the organization mentality. The impetuous response of many young people is "Up the Organization." Ecumenism in the mature style of merging middle-class institutions is not their "thing." So the question "Where do we go from here?" is a very urgent one.

It is indeed painful to witness the quick passing of the ecumenical era, to anticipate a future in which that "coming great church" announced a decade ago by leading ecumenists will simply not be. It seems, on the contrary, that the liveliest forces in our midst are pulling us into a sectarian future, leaving the ecumenical architects of yesterday to hold the bag, full of jaded models of the church of the future. There was to be a triumphal procession of a reunited Christendom back to the good old days before the schisms. Perhaps we are now paying a big price for the blasphemy of triumphalism that lurked in that kind of ecumenical scheming. That is ecumenism falling under a "theology for glory" — thinking big and building big, to keep pace with the growth rate enjoyed by other dominant institutions in America, like big business, big military, big government, big labor, big education, big ideology. So perhaps what we need is a big religion in a big-time church, to boast of a greater religious GNP. It is this big-headedness of a puffed-up church, this quantification of religion, that has poisoned the fruits of faith and turned the ecumenical movement sour. There are many vibrations, many signals, to indicate that the future of ecumenism along the path of the 1960s is a dead-end.

But an alternative future to institutional ecumenism — that is, having church functionaries maneuver their respective institutions into common structures — has not yet become clear. How can we turn off one future and prepare the way for another? Where do we go from here? The goal of the ecumenical movement must still be the unity of the church expressing itself in its universal mission. But there may be many models of unity. The basic guideline of the Reformation was this: all we are asking, all we need for the true unity of the church is the gospel. We cannot have the unity of the church at all costs. There are some conditions when, for the sake of the truth of the gospel, we must have the courage to blow the unity of the church. For where unity is not based on truth, it becomes repressive uniformity.

If the old ecumenical movement is stumbling on the rocks, we must let a new ecumenical movement take its place. The ecumenical movement must be recharged and go on, but not necessarily along the lines of the 1960s. It may sound trite to say, but we need an ecumenism of the Gospel. After all, that *is* the resource for renewing ecumenical activity with integrity.

Here we may reflect on some words of the Gospel of John.

They belong to all of us, and we can be together in just listening to them. The Gospel of John 17:20-26 is a fragment on love and unity. It is about love as being the true unity, like the love between the Father and the Son, like the love between the Son and his brothers, like the love of Christ for the world which the Father has given as the realm of his rule.

The love of Jesus is the power of true unity because it overcomes oppositions. It is the enemy of the game of solitaire, of independence, of going it alone in smug self-sufficiency. Love becomes uptight about apartheid. It becomes indignant if an individual is cut off and left to wither in isolation; it becomes angry when a person holds something back from the group as private property.

On a day of Christian unity this means that we are under the pressure of love to come out of our isolation. The true unity of love means transcending our individuality, without getting annihilated by the others. Down with uniformity; down with conformity! That is only the rule of one getting all the others under his own will. In the true unity of love the individual remains, but in a state that overcomes his isolation and separation.

Love gives us eyes to see that we can have unity without union; we can have communion without community. It's already happening. They used to say that Christians — and I said it too — had better become one church, because the world is scandalized by their divisions. I do not think, by and large, that this scandal remains. The world is not scandalized by different Christian groupings. It is getting used to the supermarket variety of things, and sort of expects that religion is like everything else — a little competition between Chevies and Buicks and Pontiacs is good, even though they are all made by the same company.

What we are experiencing in the ecumenical movement is that we can have unity without union — not that we have it now, but we may have it. In fact, we know that more union — I mean more mergers of the organizational bureaucratic sort — will not inspire more unity. We are all members of unions of one sort or another that lack the unity of spirit and love. The whole idea that we must get churches together before we can declare and share the unity of love is the real scandal. We should practice that unity of love according to the measure it lives within us. I mean, in advance of mergers and irregardless of any such plan in the future. Love and unity cannot be tied to commissions and constitutions which make up doctrinal statements only to legitimize plans of union.

Unity in love based on the Father's love for the Son, and the Son's love for the world means that we can hold communion in advance of and apart from an organized community. We do not have to be members of the same community organization to share the communion we have with each other through the Son. Here is where I do see a scandal. We have things turned upside down. Christians are moving together into the same communities, but they do not go forward in the same communion. It is this old distinction between communion *in sacris* and *in externis.* Christians can get together in external things; perhaps today we would say in secular things — eat together, study together, play together, sleep together, work together, vote together, — but they do not go all the way in worshiping together in sharing the body and blood of Christ. Why not? Does Christ forbid it? That is the scandal, not so much to outsiders, because I do not think anybody out there really cares; but it is an internal rending of the seamless robe of Christ. It is upside down, or inside out. Being in the same community is not part of the Gospel; living in the same communion is!

So we can have unity without union; we ought to have communion even without community. We have it wherever the love of Jesus drives us out of our independence into a transcending Spirit that lets us be who we are in unity with all the others whom he loves — overcoming all separations and discords through a harmony of life with life.

The ecumenical movement, the spiritual issues of unity and communion, are too important to leave to the people running things from above, standing in the way of what the Spirit is doing in the midst of his people.

On the official level we may expect that ecumenism will plunge along in the 1970s to consummate the merger plans of the sixties. But that is not where the action is. That is not where new things are coming up green in the churches. We may play the game of official ecumenism with our left hand, but the right hand is in touch with new ecumenical impulses that the Spirit of love is working in the one body of Christ. It may be a mistake to insist too vigorously on realizing the ecumenical plans for the 1960s. It may be better to back up a while in order to make more meaningful advances. There is an ecumenism born of the flesh of ecclesiastical scheming and opportunism; and there is an ecumenism born of the Spirit that moves people to faith, to hope and to love. Ecumenism that works by the planning of experts and the consequent manipulation of people is a worldly device of which we should have had enough from our secular institutions. The other ecumenism to which we are opening ourselves is more a matter of acknowledging what the Spirit does where and when he wills. It is not a spirituality strong on laying careful plans for the future; its strength is realizing the joy of the moment, living the future now even under conditions that put the squeeze on us. The emerging unity is of the Spirit, coming up from below, filling the hearts of people with love, not an ecumenism imposed from the top, pushing people into structures the experts have decided are efficient and good for people.

We are not sure of the shape of the new ecumenism, but this is a time for a more radical resourcing of the church through the gospel of love and the Spirit of unity. It is a time of new beginnings, accompanied by the death of treasured plans and fond hopes. The ecumenical assets of the World Council of Churches and the Second Vatican Council are virtually depleted. It is back to foundations, to the foundations of faith and theology. The way to go is to search the goals of the gospel. The search that is going on in the churches is the real hope for a new ecumenism Ecumenism must be born again, renewed by the power of apostolic faith and love. The time is ripening when a new birth of faith in the churches will call out for a new council of all the churches, which will signal the unity the Spirit has worked through the love that is bearing fruit.

19

The Fellowship
of Freaks

Matthew 5:1-12: "Seeing the crowds, he went up on the mountain, and when he sat down his disciples came to him. And he opened his mouth and taught them, saying:

'Blessed are the poor in spirit, for theirs is the kingdom of heaven.

'Blessed are those who mourn, for they shall be comforted.

'Blessed are the meek, for they shall inherit the earth.

'Blessed are those who hunger and thirst for righteousness, for they shall be satisfied.

'Blessed are the merciful, for they shall obtain mercy.

'Blessed are the pure in heart, for they shall see God.

'Blessed are the peacemakers, for they shall be called sons of God.

'Blessed are those who are persecuted for righteousness' sake, for theirs is the kingdom of heaven.

'Blessed are you when men revile you and persecute you and utter all kinds of evil against you falsely on my account. Rejoice and be glad, for your reward is great in heaven, for so men persecuted the prophets who were before you.' "

This is our special day in the year of the church. Perhaps none of us will ever have his very own day as a saint. At least I know I will not make it in the gallery of the church's heroes. This is the day for all the saints like us, members of a great host of uncanonized and unhaloed and fortunately yet unmartyred Christians. We are not super-saints — a long shot from it. The funny thing is — perhaps we do not even want to be.

When we were children, we used to like to talk about what we were going to be when we grew up. I cannot remember anyone of my friends saying he wanted to be a saint. The paradox was that while we admired the saints of old, we rather despised those who were trying so hard to be saints today. The old saints lived in a world of magic and miracle, their pictures painted against the golden background of an ethereal eternity. Their effect was to thrill the imagination. They were far beyond us and out of reach. We were taught the lives of the saints, starting with the twelve apostles, all making a bloody sacrifice of their lives, except for John, and then the early Christians going to the gallows or into the jaws of the lions. After Christianity became the acceptable religion of Rome, and there was no more killing of Christians, there were the monks going into the desert, starting the first communes in quest of personal holiness, practicing solitude and mortification of the flesh, pouring out penance, devoting themselves to prayer and meditation on the sacred texts. There were Pachomius, Anthony, Basil, and Augustine, saints who were fighting for the purity of the soul. Then another wave of saints came along, the great missionaries filled with the zeal to conquer the pagan world for Christ — Boniface in Germany, Patrick in Ireland, Ansgar in Scandinavia.

You know what happened — we studied the lives of the saints; we loved them and believed in them; then suddenly we came to Martin Luther and the Reformation, and we hit a drought. No more saints! Protestantism does not produce saints. What a desert, what a letdown! Instead, we learned that we are all saints. We are all saints and sinners at the same time. This was the message of Luther and the other reformers. There were the first-class Christians who were working full-time to become religious — pure and holy. And there were the second-class Christians, too busy working for a living in the world, raising crops and kids, to have much time left to devote to spiritual exercises.

Thus, the Reformation was a knock-out blow on the whole Gothic-type of Christianity. The saints were often seen as gothic-like figures, pointing ever up and up, like the highest steeples reaching to the skies. They were seen as climbing the giddy heights of perfection, working for the highest possible grades of holiness, meriting the marks that recommend a soul for an eternal sabbatical in heaven. We read about the saints and we believed in them; we traveled in Italy — Milan, Florence, and Rome — we walked around and inside the Gothic cathedrals, always with our necks cocked back so that our eyes could travel upward. But Gothic saints like Gothic cathedrals are a thing of the past.

We cannot forget that All Saints' Day is forever different because by sheer historical accident it happened to coincide with the Luther-event. Because of that event this day has become our day, a day to celebrate the grace of God which is great, not so much because it saves us *from sinning,* but more because it saves us *in our sinning*; not so much because of the few super-saints that have a big niche in the kingdom of God but because there is room for all the little ones, the poor in spirit, those who mourn in their defeat, who are not filling up a great treasury of merits and who have no extra supplements of the soul to spread around. If the grace of God is only coming along to skim off the rich cream of humanity, if it is only a blessing to those who enter the hall of fame on their heroic deeds, then there is not much hope for us.

We are going to make it by grace or we are not going to make it at all. That was Luther's insight into the gospel. With one hundred per cent of my soul, that is where I remain on All Saints' Day. I see myself and all around me in a kind of rogues' gallery. Because of the sheer unmerited love and mercy of Christ, we can enter the gallery of God's heroes, now and forevermore. That means we do not have to wait until twenty years after we are dead to learn that we have been canonized, though we have performed no miracles, founded no great institution, prayed at no great length, converted no great number of heathen, written no great spiritual classics. But for Christ's sake, we are o.k. the way we are, though there is really not much to be said for us now. We are poor in spirit; we mourn in our sins, if we are not so meek, yet we are weak, certainly not among the powerful of the earth. We are empty though we crave for righteousness, mercy, purity, and peace, and all that is great and good in the kingdom of heaven. But we do not have it all now. We experience the tension and the contradiction between what we are and who we are, between where we are and where we shall be: poor now, but then the kingdom of heaven; oppression now, but then the whole earth as the coming inheritance; hunger and thirst now, but finally a satisfying righteousness for all; rejects of the historical process now but finally a lasting status as sons of God — an enormous tension between the actual present situation and the essential future which lies hidden for us in the word of Jesus' promises. Luther saw and experienced this unbelievable tension.

We are sinful, yet holy. He saw in the church a real tension and contradiction — actually a fellowship of freaks, but essentially a communion of saints; actually divided, yet essentially one; actually very limited, yet essentially catholic and universal; actually very sinful, but essentially spotless and without blemish. The church is a split community, because it is a battleground between God's Spirit of truth and holiness and the powers of evil working death and degradation in the body of humanity. The line of God's activity does not run between a holy church and a sinful world, but right through the middle of the church and the heart of every Christian, sinful and holy at the same time — reflecting both the shadows of sin on its darker side and the light of God's grace revealing its true nature.

The church as the communion of saints has no greater and no lesser capacity for evil than other communities of the world. The church is no better and no worse. History tells us that; our own confession of the truth based on experience tells the same thing. Yet by God the church is different. We believe in the communion of saints. The saints are different; though they exist in a solidarity of suffering and sin with all other men, they are not bound together by natural birth like families, by national boundaries like countries. They are not a community of special interest, like labor unions or professional societies, like health or cultural organizations. They are united not be anything that lies within them, but only by what lies beyond them, by God's calling, election, and setting apart. The saints do not live from their own spiritual assets and moral accomplishments.

It is a liberating thought to realize that no saint ever tried to be a saint. When St. Francis bent over to kiss the leper, one can hardly imagine him saying to himself, "Here comes a leper. I know I don't like the looks or the smell of this leper, but since I want to be a saint, I can't afford to miss this opportunity. So here goes!" The saints are not self-serving persons bent on breaking all records of moral striving and attaining. The saint is not setting an unattainable example so far out of sight of ordinary Christians. Rather, the saint is giving an interpretation of the holiness and love of God at work in the everyday world of human struggling. The saint is no super-Christian, but a Christian servant. The Gothic saint is dead!

We need a new type of saint. He will not be a person off by himself in a cloistered corner, withdrawn from the world, spinning his own little prayer wheel, competing to outdo himself in spiritual exercises. We need worldly saints, saints in the world, not with eyes looking to the heavens, but bent down in sharing and bearing the burdens of men on earth. We need saints, not as illustrations of how far a single Christian can go in getting to heaven by climbing a ladder of personal spirituality, but as interpretations of Christ stooping to serve in the fellowship of human sin and suffering. Then I believe we will understand the old saints better. We can remove the film of dust and grime that has legendarily settled on the figures of the saints. We can take them down from their

Gothic steeples and see them not as saints way ahead of us drawing near to God, but as sinners very close to us in whom God is drawing near to men in the fellowship of their sin and suffering. Because this is so by the word of the Gospel, this is a day for all of us. We can feel glad and comfortable being counted among the saints of this day.

Part Four

The Whole
Man

20

Climbing
the Ladder of
Religion

Acts 17:22-31: "So Paul, standing in the middle of
the Areopagus, said: 'Men of Athens, I perceive that
in every way you are very religious. For as I passed
along, and observed the objects of your worship, I
found also an altar with this inscription, "To an
unknown god." What therefore you worship as
unknown, this I proclaim to you. The God who made
the world and everything in it, being Lord of heaven
and earth, does not live in shrines made by man, nor
is he served by human hands, as though he needed
anything, since he himself gives to all men life and
breath and everything. And he made from one every
nation of men to live on all the face of the earth,
having determined allotted periods and the boundaries of their habitation, that they should seek God,
in the hope that they might feel after him and find
him. Yet he is not far from each one of us, for
    "In him we live and move and have our being";
    'as even some of your poets have said,
    "for we are indeed his offspring."
    'Being then God's offspring, we ought not to think
that the Deity is like gold, or silver, or stone, a
representation by the art and imagination of man.
The times of ignorance God overlooked, but now he
commands all men everywhere to repent, because he
has fixed a day on which he will judge the world in
righteousness by a man whom he has appointed, and
of this he has given assurance to all men by raising
him from the dead. ' "

The apostle Paul was standing in the Areopagus — a kind of civic plaza — in Athens. He was a Jew, ready to preach a sermon to Greeks; he was the only Christian there, looking out upon a pagan audience. The first thing that came to his mind was to establish a point of contact with these people in Athens. "I see, you are a very religious people." I see your objects of worship and this altar to "an unknown God." Paul knew about their religion; he had studied Greek mythology and Plato's philosophy of religion. He knew of the salvation scheme in this religion. The Orphic myth was widespread. Man is made of body and soul, and the soul is the real self that comes from God, the divine part, the divine spark, in man. That soul has fallen into an earthly, material, and sensual body. That body is the prison-house of the soul; that soul is a light buried in the darkness of the body. The whole point of religion is to free the soul, to break its earthly fetters, and to help it ascend to the level of the divine from whence it came.

So I see, you are a very religious people, Paul said. You are busy at purifying the soul from its defilement in the body. You have your objects of worship — your altars to remind you of your heavenly home and eternal values. You have learned from your greatest philosopher that famous allegory about the cave. Surely you have read Plato's *Republic.* Isn't what Plato said still true, that we are like men sitting in a cave? All we can see around us are shadows, shadows on the wall of this underground cave. Some people take these shadows to be the realities. But we know, the soul knows, that everything in this world is only a shadow, and that the realities lie in an upper world, in another realm. The whole point and purpose of religion is to get us to ascend to the eternal realities beyond this world of shadows and senses, to lift the soul like an oyster outside its shell of this material body.

Paul had an understanding and a respect for this religion. He showed neither scorn nor arrogance. He knew that religion is where God meets man, where heaven and earth come together and touch, where the longing in man to be in union with God is most deeply felt. Paul was here being a witness to the gnosticisms that were swarming around the dying world of antiquity. In this world view, religion is like a ladder that reaches to heaven, mounting up from this earthly cave. Getting to heaven by climbing a ladder is one of the most ancient and widespread symbols. One of the most popular symbols in the Middle Ages was Jacob's ladder. Perhaps you have even sung that song, "We are climbing Jacob's ladder." It continues, "Every rung goes higher, higher."

Paul himself had been a very religious man; he had been climbing his own kind of heavenly ladder, going up each rung of the law. He had pursued the works of the law which would lead him up the staircase of the righteousness of God. When Paul said, "I perceive that in every way you are very religious," he meant that these people were good at climbing the ladder into the mysteries of the deities, represented by gold or silver or some other metal.

There were seven rungs in the ceremonial ladder in the mysteries of Mithra. The first was made of lead, for the heaven of the planet Saturn; the second was made of tin, for Venus; the third of bronze for Jupiter; the fourth of iron for Mercury; the fifth of "monetary alloy" for Mars; the sixth of silver for the moon, and the seventh of gold for the sun. The eighth stood for the sphere of the fixed stars. By going up this ceremonial ladder, the religious man was supposed to pass through the seven heavens, thus lifting his soul into the empyrean, into the ultimate heaven.

There may be many different kinds of ladders, different kinds of staircases, different ways of making the ascent of the soul into the ultimate heaven of some mind-blowing bliss. Theodore Roszak writes in his latest book, *Where the Wasteland Ends,*

> So now we see (in this age of Big Science and Big Technology) a revival of mystical religion, primitive lore and ritual, occultism . . . . An increasing number of people in urban-industrial society will take their bearings in life from the I Ching and the signs of the zodiac, from yoga and strange contemporary versions of shamanic tradition.

It is the revival, says Roszak, of that old-time religion, that universal gnosticism which makes a vertical takeoff into some heavenly realm of visionary beatitude.

No wonder that millions of copies of *Jonathan Livingston Seagull* have been sold in the last two years. I have seen only one TV studio show in my life; that was the Dick Cavett show last summer. The guest for the day happened to be Richard Bach, the author of this best-selling bird-book, latest representative of this universal primitive mysticism that beats in the human heart, longing to escape on the wings of a metaphysical or mystical bird. It strikes a vulnerable spot in our weary urban Hyde Park hearts, with all the filth and crime and war and corruption too big to miss. Who wouldn't long to fly away from it all? A bad book full of blathering nonsense, some say. But it is the old spiritualism, the fascinating gnosticism, the perennial temptation, to let our souls migrate to a heavenly city, like the city of the sky which Aristophanes' birds of old tried to build in the cloud cuckooland. This is the religion of the seagull, the free and unfettered flight of the bird into the skies, the religion of the vision-flight that associates divinity with height, levity, loftiness, weightlessness, climbing and soaring, until the rational mind drifts off into the inaccessible realm of the unknown and nameless void.

Paul is looking out upon all this sweet and swinging religion, thinking, "Do I have anything in my own experience to help me understand what I see? Indeed, I've been climbing the ladder too, the ladder of the law according to works; I've been trying to reach perfection and the righteousness of God. But it didn't work for me." It's just a different ladder, and it won't get you to where you're trying to go.

At that point Paul wades into his sermon, preaching the gospel of the God who is very near. Paul's gospel is a kind of memorandum to the people of Athens and to every religious people, including Christian people today: Don't let your religion take you up the heavenly ladder. Is your religion a ladder going in the wrong direction? Is it taking you away from the action? Taking you out of this world? Is it a vision-ary ascent of the soul out of the body? Is it an altar to an unknown god?

But this I proclaim: God is not far away at the top of a staircase, not a voice from heaven, coaxing you to climb one rung at a time. God is an earth-man, a down-to-earth man. Heaven has joined the business of this earth and mingles in the affairs of human beings. The song by Christina Rossetti that we sing in the Christmas season puts it well: "Love came down at Christmas . . . Love incarnate, Love divine."

The current of the incarnation comes down, always comes down. "Not an ascent from body to spirit, but the descent of spirit into body," cries Norman Brown. The French have a saying, "To fit neatly into one's skin." This all means that the body is a beautiful and comfortable place for the spirit; this means that the body is not the partition-wall between God and man, not a hindrance to communion with God. Celsus, the great third-century pagan enemy of Christianity in Origen's time, ridiculed Christians because they had a *desider-ium corporis* — that is, a love for their bodies. Paradoxically, this pagan philosopher had a better grasp of the gospel at this point than Origen himself, who was so bothered by his body that he became a eunuch.

When Paul speaks about the God who is near to each one of us, whose offspring we are and by whose righteousness we shall be judged, he has his mind on that appointed man. In this sermon he did not even mention his name, but he is that man of whom God has approved by raising him in the body from the dead. He is the man Jesus of Nazareth — a real man of history, a real man of flesh and blood, of pain and sorrow. Here is where the staircase comes down to earth and gets fastened there. Here is where the ladder to heaven becomes rather the tree of life with roots growing deeper into this earth. Here is where the tree becomes a cross, and here in the cross is where eternity and time meet. Time is not here collapsed and transformed into eternity, but eternity is trans-formed into time, reaching out to all corners.

It has been very difficult in two thousand years of Christian history to keep our faith really down-to-earth. We are like the children of Israel in Isaiah's time — very impressed, even seduced by the idols of our neighbors and by the attractive gods they serve. We like to be as religious as they, to take our turn at climbing the sacred ladders, getting our share of peak experiences.

If Christians had not been found clinging to their religious ladders, suspended halfway between heaven and earth, there would hardly have been these outbursts of irreligion that have become menacingly angry and widespread in modern times, particularly where the churches once were dominant. Even Julian Huxley expresses alarm at the fact that the decline of religion in our Western nations is leaving a vacuum of unfilled needs. These needs are not going to be filled by more science, more technology, and more economic growth. But is not irreligion now a mass movement that is firmly established on its own?

It has been shown by a sociologist Colin Campbell, in *Toward a Sociology of Irreligion,* that some of the main springs of modern irreligiosity are the religious excesses of Christians themselves; persecution, bloody religious wars, fanaticism, revivalistic emotionalism. If such things are produced by religion, then for God's sake and for the sake of human sanity and our earthly welfare, we have to set up counter-religious movements. And we have them! I think Paul would have placed his gospel rather on the side of these counter-religious movements, these protests against all the religious ladders that lead us into a dizzy foggy no-man's land, halfway between heaven and earth. We have no business climbing Jacob's ladder. We should stay with the life of the spirit in the body of mankind here on earth. The poet Rilke was an earth-and body-mystic, and he said, "The body becomes a spiritual fact."

If Christians had stayed with this life, if they had not been hanging onto their ladders, it would hardly have occurred to Karl Marx to call the Christian hope "pie in the sky." Only a theology that has betrayed the down-to-earth gospel of that appointed man Jesus could be called an ideology of the ruling classes, who enjoy privileged status in the status quo. The great attacks on religion coming from Marx and Feuerbach and Freud and Sartre are an open warfare against religion, but, mind you, against the religion of the ladders that carry us away from our humanity, from these earthen vessels, these beautiful claypots in which God has poured the vitalities of heaven and the animating impulses of his living Spirit.

It is all right to be religious, but don't let it take you up the heavenly ladder. Stay with life and stick with the affairs that make up the daily stuff of life. Martin Luther had also tried his hand on the rungs of the ladder ascending to heaven. Like Paul, he tried the way of the works of the law, trying to gain a righteousness that would count before God in heaven. He tried the way of good works and the winning of merits. But when he fell off his ladder, he found that good works are good for nothing in the currency exchange of heaven. They are nonnegotiable. God doesn't need them but your neighbor does. As Paul says, "God is not served by human hands, as though he needed anything." Rather, Luther found, God's works come down from above, and his blessings open up heaven for us in this earthly existence.

Luther also tried the ladder of speculation. When he was in the monastery, he studied the devotional writings of the mystics, who wrote of the itinerary of the soul in its ascent to heaven. But all this speculation on the majesty of God, this plunging into the unsearchable mystery of God and the unfathomable divine abyss — this is following after the lusts of the Spirit. These lusts of the Spirit are much more danger-ous and damnable than the lusts of the flesh — as tricky as they are. God is not reached by the soul going up a *scala sancta* — a holy staircase — of mystical or natural theology. "Oh, what a ridiculous thing," Luther said, "that the one God, the high Majesty, should be a man."

Because the incarnation means the nearness of God in that appointed man Jesus, we are the heirs and practitioners of a body spirituality, not a ladder spirituality. When Luther got down off his high ladder, he shocked the world by getting married. He had discovered that the Bible is a down-to-earth book, not a system of ladders or a mystical manual on how to ascend elsewhere. He had discovered that the gospel is a down-to-earth message of a God who comes where people are, not inviting them to find him elsewhere. He had discovered that the real life of the Spirit is not lived in a half-hearted commitment to this earth, but it means real freedom to take it all in. He believed that God is coming to judge the world; so he reasoned, why waste your life climbing some ladder? If God is coming, then a person ought to be found living as God intended him to live on this earth, like a human being, doing human things, like getting married and having children. If God is near, that's no cause to be doing conspicuously pious things; he can see right through you. He wants to find you doing earthly things. One of Luther's students asked him — this has been quoted many times — "If the end of the world were to come tomorrow, what would you do?" Luther said, "I would go out in the garden and plant a tree."

Of course, Paul and Luther were following the line that Jesus walked on earth. Jesus was the man appointed to show us the way and by whom we shall be judged. He did not walk around with his eyeballs rolling to the skies and a holy lilt in his gait; he had no halo around his head. He was a plain down-to-earth man, calling people not to join a religious crusade, not to devote themselves to a religious quest for transcendence that might lead them elsewhere from where they are. He calls them to discipleship right now. Not a religious quest but Christian discipleship is the thing, Bonhoeffer said, and that is doing your spiritual thing right in your tracks, like the Samaritan on the road to Jericho.

If Luther shocked the world by getting married, Jesus shocked the pious people of his day by eating and drinking with publicans and sinners. If Luther said he'd go out and plant a tree, Jesus said, I'm going out to heal a leper and help a lame man walk. He turned the ladders of religion upside down, saying, so nobody could mistake his meaning, "The Sabbath is made for man and not man for the Sabbath." Jesus got himself killed for what he said and did. Of course, he could have avoided this inconvenience, if only he would have kept himself to a religious ladder, and devoted himself to spiritual athletics, teaching others how to climb each rung higher, higher.

But Jesus was not a holy man; he was not a saint. We don't call him St. Jesus. He did not excel at climbing a staircase. He was nailed to a cross, and they called to him to come down from the cross, if he were truly the Son of God. There in that weakness, there in that suffering, in that helplessness, God has committed himself to the fate and the finitude, to the pain and the suffering, of this real world. That means that we are not living with shadows — we are not shadowboxing — but we are the realities and the game of life is for real. We are not in a cave; we are in the real world. We are not in a religious quest that leads us elsewhere. We are not seeking God in our souls; we are following Christ in our bodies. When we speak of transcendence, which is the watchword of the romantic revival of our time, we mean incarnational transcendence. We are not in quest of an otherworldly, supernatural transcendence beyond this earth, outside our bodies, in some timeless eternity where nothing much ever happens. Then we would be going back up the heavenly ladder. We follow the incarnational current that makes its way through this earth, that is, the forward-moving river of life itself. We are not taking a trip into the depths of the unknown, in search of some real self inside the human onion, in search of some vanishing identity that bears no name. That is only the latest religious gimmick, which no longer believes in heaven and the starry skies above, but dips rather into the murky depths below, in search of some weightless and nameless identity in the abyss of chaotic feelings.

Jesus lived an open and public life, not looking for meaning deep down or high up in peak experiences, not being on a staircase himself. In doing this he declared as God's appointed man: "It's okay to live this life. We have God's permission to live it freely. There is nothing wrong with the body as the place to do it. Stick to history! You can't do your thing elsewhere; you must do it here and now. And there is no magic way, no bag of tricks. But just the human way. Because that is God's chosen way." Truth comes riding on a donkey. I don't know who said that, but that is the human, incarnational way of God. There's no prize at the top of the staircase. But there is real life in the body of Christ. That is the source of the new identity of all the members who make it their center of gravity.

As I was thinking about this down-to-earth gospel that Paul preached to the religious men of Athens, I came across this word from Dostoievsky in a Sunday bulletin: "Let the person who desires to see the living God face to face seek him not in the empty firmament of his mind, but in human love." That is the love of God that became human in that appointed man Jesus.

21

The Coming
of the Spirit
in the Body

Rom. 8:11: "If the Spirit of him who raised Jesus from the dead dwells in you, he who raised Christ Jesus from the dead will give life to your mortal bodies also through his Spirit which dwells in you."

1 Cor. 6:13: "[The body is meant] for the Lord, and the Lord for the body."

The Advent season is a time of waiting. But what are we waiting for? We are waiting for something to happen, someone to come! We are waiting for Christ to come. But he has already come. So it must mean that we are waiting for him to come again, and to come soon. That is the element of urgency, of expectancy. But where and how does he come so soon? I've wondered about that, and so have you. He comes in the Spirit; that is how he comes again and soon. But where does he come? He comes in the body. That is where we are. I want to proclaim that the Advent of Christ is the coming of the Spirit in the body.

Christianity is a religion of the concrete body, of the coming of the Spirit of Christ in the body. The unique thing about Christianity is not that it talks a lot about spirit. Religion had been spiritual enough before the coming of Christ. With the coming of Christ, the Spirit and all spiritual language would be hooked up with the body. There can be no separation of soul from body, or of the Spirit of Christ from the body of humanity — your body and mine, our concrete bodies.

Paul said, "The body is . . . for the Lord, and the Lord for the body." The body is that concrete piece of earthly reality which we ourselves are. The body is the theater of the coming of the Lord. It is a temptation for all religions to be spiritual, to be spirit religions, to dedicate the soul or the spirit to God. In the Christian gospel, it is the body that is the living sacrifice to God; that is "our spiritual service."

The religious view is that God claims our spirits; let our bodies go hang. The Christian view is that the Spirit claims our bodies. The body is the temple of the Holy Spirit. The Spirit identifies the kingdom of Christ with one's own body. Don't expect a future kingdom that is not seeking to reign already in your own mortal body. One of the most ancient Christian heresies is that Christianity is such a spiritual religion, that the abuse and the neglect of the body could be approved. It's the spirit, or the soul, that counts. That is why the years of news about the body-count in Vietnam was a blasphemy against Christ and a sin against the Holy Spirit who comes in the body, or not at all!

The body is the theater of the kingdom of God and the advent of the Spirit of Christ. The moment you take the Spirit out of the body, or place it alongside the body, you reduce the body to a mechanism or a vegetable, dead in itself, a meaningless carcass with artificial life, a sham imitation of the glory of God in man. This is a terribly serious human problem today, when on the one side our bodies become food for the war machine, chewed-up flesh to satisfy the insatiable appetite of the dragon in our midst; on the other side there are those who blow their minds to struggle free of their bodies, turned off by a society which demands the total worship of both body and soul.

There is not that much difference between the war lords who sacrifice our bodies on the altar of national pride or industrial progress and the priests of the youth culture who deaden the body through the psychedelic sacraments, drugs, to let the spirits soar into dreamy regions beyond the body. They both hate the body, both polarized sides — those who bleed the bodies and those who blow their minds. Both are cults that despise the body.

Christianity is a religion with a lovely body-accent. To be or not to be, that is a question of the body. Some materialist, I think it was first Ludwig Feuerbach, thought he was uttering some gosh-awful heresy, when he said, *"Man ist was er isst."* Man is what he eats. Little did he know that he hit the nail right on the head. Jesus said, "This is my body." To eat the body is to participate in life eternal. There is no way to God, and no way from God to man, except in the body and through a body ecstasy. Luther said, "You can never draw the Son of God too deeply into human flesh." Christian faith is violated when it becomes too spiritual, not when it becomes too somatic.

When we talk about the body, we are talking about food, eating and drinking. It was by eating that man got into trouble, according to the myth of the fall of man. It was by eating that the Corinthian Christians betrayed the body of Christ, because they failed to respect all the poorer members who belonged to the one and same body. And it is by eating that redemption comes. Unless you eat the flesh of the Son of Man and drink his blood, you won't have any life in you. By eating, that is, by the bread which we break, we become participants in the body of Christ. This is not just a metaphor, as Zwingli thought. It is metamorphosis, as Luther thought. There is a real coming, a real presence of the Christ in the present.

A belief in the body is a belief in the power of bread to make alive, through the physical event of eating, which is the most spiritual event we know in the Christian doctrine of action.

The common view is that what we eat is changed into what we are — the meat and the potatoes, the fish and the chips. The Christian view is that we are converted into what we eat

— the body of Christ, of which we become living members. Eschatology, the coming of the kingdom of God, is a real coming in the body of Christ, through our eating and drinking. Do not make the kingdom so far off and futuristic that you forget it is a coming kingdom, a real advent, that we celebrate in the breaking of bread and the drinking of wine.

We are broken bodies; we are fractured human beings. The gospel of Advent is this. There is a breakthrough of the Spirit in our breaking of bread. The liturgical word for the breaking of bread is the fraction — the fraction of the body of Christ, for the fractured bodies of men, mere fractions of the real humanity we are destined to become in the true body of Christ, the one real Man for all seasons.

What does this reverence for the body mean? It means to locate the kingdom in our own bodies, to look for the work of the Spirit in that concrete piece of the world that is our body. This body of ours is one and the same stuff as our natural environment, the air we breathe, and the water we drink. We have to take this quite literally in order that we might see it also symbolically. The water we drink is the same water with which we are baptized, the means of purifying and regenerating our deadened selves. The air we breathe is the wind that blows into our bodies, the Spirit, the *ruach,* the *pneuma,* the very breath to support life. This is why the fight for our environment today is a spiritual fight, a fight for the advent of the Spirit in our mortal bodies.

There can be no separation of Spirit and body. There is a coming of the Spirit into the body, not an ascent of the soul out of the body, as in other religions. The true meaning of Christianity must be bodily meaning, for the reason that the Word of God comes in a body; the resurrection of Christ is a spiritual body; the church is the body of Christ; our eating bread together is a communion of the body of Christ, and we are promised the redemption of our bodies in the resurrection to lasting life. This is a beautiful body mysticism.

Here must be the clue for our way of life. What you do with your body is where you are, where your head is. It has to do with sex and politics, with what we do with out bodies privately and politically. As sex enables the union of two bodies, two persons knowing each other, so the Eucharist is a marriage union of Christ with his church. And the body politic of which we are a part is the place where we are to worship God with our bodies. It is the battlefield of the two opposing power systems, one unto life, the other unto death, each contending for the rule of the total body.

The abuse and hatred of the body in our dominant culture have also slipped into the counter-culture, also shaping the attitudes and actions of Christians. Abbie Hoffman blows into Chicago, announcing he's not had a bath in three months. Antonius, the disciple of Simeon the Stylite, was praising his saintly model, when he said, "When he walks, vermin drop from his body." He spent one summer, not on the lake tanning in the sunshine, but digging a hole in the dirt and burying himself up to his head each day. Those filthy old monks were trying their level best to be good athletes of God; but they blew it, because they did not let the kingdom come in this world, that concrete part of the world that is the body. It is in this body of ours that the coming of the Spirit can work a new awareness, sharpening our senses, so we become more sensible and more sensitive as we meet each other, bumping into each other's bodies, touching and being touched, without hurting or being hurt, and as we greet each other this morning in the One Body which can heal and unite all men.

22

The Glory
of Flesh and
Blood

John 1:14: "And the Word became flesh and dwelt among us, full of grace and truth; we have beheld his glory, glory as of the only Son from the Father."

The theme of my meditation is the glory of man, the glory of God in man, in that true and perfect man Jesus. My theme is the glory of the infinite in and through the finite. In the old language of Reformation theology, the good fathers expressed this theme in the Latin phrase: *finitum capax infiniti* — the finite is capable of the infinite. This was a theological statement of the glory of the incarnation: the Word has become flesh and blood, and the glory of God shines through the body-and-blood-reality of a person. Now I could stop here, because that's all that I really want to say. But I won't, because I want to relate it to our present situation.

Glory is a word of *awe*; it is a word that evokes a sense of majesty, of something of weighty importance. There is the glory of riches, the glory of a mighty army and royal figures. There is the glory of the temple and of the ark of the covenant. There is the glory of God as a numinous and luminous presence, as a fiery flash on Mt. Sinai, or as sacred presence around the tabernacle. In all of these the glory of God is connected with places and things. No man can see God and live, but his glory can glance off something, and you know you stand in the environment of his presence in fear and trembling. For example: there is Moses and the burning bush; there is Paul on the Damascus road; there is poor Uzzah who touched the ark of the covenant and dropped dead; there are the angels walking up and down the heavenly ladder singing songs — the glory of God was shining through these events, and the people who saw its reflected light were blinded or blessed.

But, of course, we don't really have experiences quite like that; there are those who say that it's because of this secular age in which we live. We were deluged by secular theology for a while, and many people are convinced that religion is dead. That's why we don't have burning bushes, six-winged cherubim and a feeling for the *mysterium tremendum*. There may be a lot of truth to that. But I would like to say that, for us, the glory of God has not disappeared because of our secular age. It has been redefined; it has been relocated; it is no longer an Olympian type of glory, where we have to reach up to high and mighty images of greatness to grasp a glimmering of the divine light and glory. It is no longer a ritualistic and religious type of glory, where it comes and goes, like a flash of lightning and only a few heroes of faith get in on it.

The Word has become flesh and dwells among us. The glory of God is in a human face and shines through the activities of a human heart. The glory of God comes to stay, to tabernacle among us, in a real presence in and through the common and daily forms of our living together, of our eating and drinking together. This is the glory of the incarnation, that God is no longer on top of a mountain, no longer making an oracular communication from on high, nor dwelling in unapproachable light. Jesus was the most approachable man of his day but he poured his glory into the finite form of human flesh and blood, into the daily needs of something to eat and something to drink, of bread and wine, of something to taste and something to feel.

I said that we have been deluged by a decade of secular theology, which said that God is dead or gone, and there is no glory to awaken awe, fascination, and to inspire praise and worship. Now, perhaps, we are going to be swamped by a decade of religious theology. We will be seeing people, and some theologians among them, poking around here and there for a glimpse of the glory of God. They will be going back to the Olympian type of glory. They will bow before idols enshrouded in mystery; they will go from magic to witch-craft; they will again wander in the holy groves and gather up holy stones. Then we will be able to say with St. Paul: we see that you are a very religious people. Myth and magic, mystery and ecstasy, even occultism and satanism will be swirling around us with dizzying fascination. Many Christians will be tempted to chase after these false, phony, and fascin-ating fairy tales about where the gods are in our time.

Whether the soul of a person is suffocated by the stale air of secularism or saturated by the intoxicating wine of reli-gious enthusiasm, he is going to miss the new definition of glory, the new demonstration of glory in the human face and human hand of Jesus of Nazareth. Theodore Roszak has written a new book, *Where the Wilderness Ends*. He predicts that, after an overdose of science and technology, we will be glad to get back to religion, mystical feelings, and nature worship. He is counting on man's religious nature to rise again. He says it is already happening. But in getting back to all this religion, we run the danger of overshooting the mark of the incarnation. We will see people returning to that Olympian view of the glory of God; we will see people again building a Tower of Babel, trying to reach the glory of God in the skies, in the lofty regions where the gods dwell above us. We will see people trying to deal with God at the level of God. They will miss the glory of the incarnation, that God has chosen to deal with us at the human level.

Perhaps we are somewhat relieved that religious impulses are finding their way back into our secular world; it is per-haps the swinging of the pendulum back to a more normal state. But we should not mistake all this religion, all this religiosity, for the really Christian thing.

The Christian thing is that you will find God in humanness and personalness, that God manifests his glory in his Son, who is really a human individual. He asks us to find his glory in his Son, who is really a human individual. He asks us to find his glory and his majesty in the form of human flesh and blood. We worship God as a man-sized God, flesh of our flesh and bone of our bone. Because God glorifies man in the incarnation, we all become glorified by sharing the humanity of his body and blood. You can say today, as you eat his body and drink his blood, that you are being glorified. I am being glorified, not by religious experience, not by becoming more pious than the pious, although we are free to take all that into the bargain, just as we are free also to share in the secular experiences of our day; but whether we are more secular or whether we are more religious in our style, we are being glorified in our humanity. That God has glorified himself in the humanity of Jesus means that there is no greater gift that we can make to another than the gift of ourselves. There is no greater gift that a husband can give to his wife than his humanity, all the flesh that is his, all the blood that is his, all the love that he can show through his flesh and blood. There is no greater gift that a wife can give to her husband than the entire beautiful body that is hers and all the love that she can express through it; no greater unity than the unity of God with humanity in Jesus Christ, and of Christ with all his brothers and sisters through sharing his body and blood, and of us with each other through joining in eating and drinking. Because of all this, there is no greater purpose in life than to share in the mission of God to glorify mankind. All the religions say that the greatest thing is for man to glorify God. We believe on account of Christ that the greatest thing is for God to glorify man, and he is doing it. He is a very human God. A philosopher has said that man is the measure of all things. St. John has been called the theologian among the evangelists; he says that man is the measure of God. The Word has become flesh, and the glory of God has been seen in a human being.

Luther loved this verse more than anything else; he said, "I know of no God but the one who gave himself for me. Isn't that a great thing that God is human, that God gives himself to us human beings as a human being, as a man gives himself to his wife and is hers. But if God is ours, all things are ours." We do not have to flee from man to God and reach up to an otherworldly glory; God has reached down to us, and has achieved the glorification of man. We can stick to the task of being and becoming really human and personal, so that we don't try to jump out of our skins, or leap out of history, in chasing after the glory of God in heavenly places and missing the glory of the humanity of God in the earthly Jesus Christ.

23

On

Leaving Your

Country

Gen. 12:1-3: Now the Lord said to Abram, "Go from your country and your kindred and your father's house to the land that I will show you. And I will make of you a great nation, and I will bless you, and make your name great, so that you will be a blessing. I will bless those who bless you, and him who curses you I will curse; and by you all the families of the earth will bless themselves."

One of the hottest issues in America today is the question of amnesty. You know what that means — many young people have left America in protest against the Vietnam War. Amnesty would mean that the young men can return now after the war is over, and we will be reconciled to them. Amnesty means we want them back — from Sweden and Switzerland, from England and France, from Hong Kong and Singapore. These young people left America because they experienced a command, an inner voice, which said, "Go from your country and your fellow countrymen, and leave your father's house and your school and your job."

I point this out, not to settle the issue of amnesty or to make a political speech, but to ask: What would it take for you to leave your country? What did it take for Abraham to leave his country? What did it take for my father to leave his country? Except for the Indians and except for those shipped over here as slaves, every one of us had fathers or forefathers who experienced the command to Abraham in some form or other: "Leave your country and strike out on a new path, cutting ties with the past and opening up a new line to the future. Follow your dreams, and don't get caught in your nightmares." So what would it take for you to leave your country?

As Americans we are bitterly divided today on the meaning and mission of America. You have read the bumper stickers, "Love it or leave it!" But Abraham left it, because there was something more important to him than patriotism, blind loyalty, and love of country. There is a higher command! There is a higher loyalty! Each one of us is thrown into the world in a special place and of a particular race. We start out in life with a certain blood origin, a certain clan and class and tribe and family, and a certain language and dialect, certain manners and mores, even a certain religion and type of morality. That is the starting point. We all start from somewhere. Abraham started in Ur of the Chaldees; he left his country and became the father of many nations. Jesus started in Bethlehem, and now he has a community in his name in every continent, in every country, and a book about him in every language, and almost every dialect. So it is not where you started, but where you are going. Now it is up to each one of us to know his origins and be proud of them, and not to be ashamed of where he comes from. It also means not to be tied to the past, not to be in bondage to the soil of your birthplace or the prejudices of your blood origin or the politics of your country and the blind spots of your religious heritage. It means *to become free.*

We are going through a crisis of national identity and destiny in America today. The word of God to Abraham is still true for us. Get our from your country. We can take that in symbolic terms! It does not mean for us that we have to go to Europe or Africa or somewhere else. It does not mean a trip we take with our bodies. It is a soul-trip, a trip of heads and hearts, an adventure of mind and faith, the acquisition of new and higher loyalties. We must get together and find out what the command to Abraham means in our time and in our nation.

Abraham Lincoln said in the Gettysburg Address: "Our fathers brought forth on this continent a new nation, conceived in liberty and dedicated to the proposition that all men are created equal." Then he went on to say, "Now we are engaged in a great civil war, testing whether that nation or any nation so conceived and so dedicated can long endure." In a real sense we are still in that civil war, still testing whether the American dream has a chance of coming true, still testing whether that dream points to a reality that is worth leaving one's country for, still worth living and dying for.

What does it mean to get out from one's country, to follow the command of God to Abraham, at this time in the history of America? It means that we have to renew the vision and awaken from a nightmare that has fallen upon us. Especially as Christian people who are sons of Abraham, not according to the flesh, but according to faith and the promises of God, we have to lead the way to a new vision and a new reality.

This means that we must be aware of three steps: *where we have come from,* that is our beginnings; *where we are now,* that is, at this time of national crisis; and third, *where we are going,* that is, our mission as Christians in the world.

First of all, where we have come from, our beginnings! Our fathers came to this country to found a nation conceived in liberty. One Frenchman as early as 1782 wrote, and he expressed the feelings of many, "Here individuals of all nations are melted together into a new race of men, whose labors and posterity will one day cause great changes in the world." And at the beginning of this century a Jewish immigrant wrote, "America is God's crucible, the great melting pot where all races of Europe are merging and reforming — Germans and Frenchmen, Irishmen and Englishmen, Jews and Russians — into the crucible with you all! God is making the American!"

This has been called by sociologists the "myth of the melting pot." Every foreigner, every new group coming to our shores, was to be put into the melting pot, stirred around for a few years in the public school, and then come out waving an American flag. In Detroit, Henry Ford hired lots of immigrants to build the model-T and the model-A Fords. He placed all these foreigners working for him in the Ford English School to make them into solid American citizens. At graduation time the administrators of this school invented a unique ceremony. Let me quote from the text in the archives of the Ford Motor Company.

> Not long ago [it states] this school graduated over five hundred men. Commencement exercises were held in the largest hall in the city [of Detroit]. On the stage was represented an immigrant ship. In front of it was a huge melting pot. Down the gang plank came the members of the class dressed in their national garbs and carrying luggage such as they carried when they landed in this country. Then the teachers began to stir the contents of the pot with long ladles. Presently the pot began to boil over and out came the men dressed in their best American clothes and waving American flags.

That is the myth of the melting pot. It is to the credit of the leaders of the black liberation movement — Martin Luther King, Malcom X, Cassius Clay, Lew Alcindor, and many others — that this myth of the melting pot is no longer accepted as the true dream of America. No one wants to get melted down in anybody else's pot. That is the root of the new consciousness. The meaning of America is not in melting down our differences into the mass of like-minded people, all being, doing, thinking, and learning the same thing. So that takes us to the second point — where we are now at this time of national crisis.

We are at the point of rejecting false gods, especially the false god that lingers on in the myth of the melting pot. We are sifting the American dream. We are testing what this nation is all about. Many do not believe that the greatness of this new nation that our forefathers brought forth on this continent lies in military strength, in the arrogance of power, of imperial ambition, of economic materialism and expansionism — and along with these things the orgies of violence they produce on the battlefield and domestically in our homes and in the streets. He who lives by the gun shall die by the gun. We do not use swords in our time. We have to know where we are before we can get going again. There is something very wrong with a nation in which young people want to change their names and disguise their ancestry — Cassius Clay becomes Muhammad Ali; Lew Alcindor becomes Abdul Kareem Jabbar, etc. — and others are made so to hate themselves that they run and hide in sex, drugs, and alcohol.

Alienation, Jules Pfeiffer says, is when your country is at war and you pray for the other side to win. The American dream has become for many a nightmare. Our fathers dreamed of a society free of hunger, disease, and poverty, but all of these we have a hundredfold. We dreamed of technology as a tool to ease the pains and sufferings of our people, and increase the pleasure and comforts. But what does it really profit a nation to gain the moon and suffer the loss of its soul? What does it profit a people to live in the space age, knowing more and more about the heavenly bodies, but still living in the Stone Age in terms of knowing our neighbors and caring for our earthly bodies? What does it profit if our heads get swollen and our hearts begin to shrink?

That brings us to the third point: Where are we going? What does the command to Abraham mean to us as Christians who live in America — to go from our homeland, to leave our father's house, and the little gods of blood and soil, of racial prejudice and nationalistic arrogance. We are to go with the promise: in you all the families of the earth shall be blessed. That promise points to Jesus Christ. There is a line of promise from Abraham to Jesus Christ. He is now the basis of our hope that all the families of the earth shall be blessed. He is the good news, that however badly the dream of our fathers is turning out, whatever the nightmares and the crises of the present, we do not cop-out or drop out, because we have reason to live by promise and by hope.

We are children of the promise to Abraham. We are not satisfied with where we have been, and we cannot return to our beginnings. We cannot settle down in the present, in the attitude of despair and hopelessness. As children of promise we do not live in the past or settle for the present; we live by hope and trust in the promises that were given to Abraham and ratified in the life and death of Jesus Christ. We must walk the line from Abraham to Jesus Christ, which is the line of promise that points to a new homeland. We are on our way to a new homeland. Our nation is not the last stop, nor do we defend it at all costs as though there is nothing greater and beyond.

We live for all people; we are international as Christians. Our nation says we have enemies; as Christians our enemies have been declared by Christ to be our friends. We are lovers of humanity and friends of all peoples, of every tribe and of every tongue, of every class and every color. There is no one superior by birth or origin. We are all one and together equal in Christ, who shows no prejudice against anyone, and no partiality for anyone. That is the challenge of the promise to hear the command to Abraham, to go from your homeland, to seek a new homeland that is truly free and free for all, a homeland in which freedom rings out, not as a boastful political slogan of one side of the world, calling itself the "free world," but a lived experience of each person in every corner of the world. To go out from your country means to live beyond the borders of your own nation, to extend the embrace of peace to all, especially to the so-called enemies. It takes no special grace to love your friends. Jesus said, "Love your enemies and pray for those who curse you."

As believers in Jesus Christ, we believe in a new humanity; we believe in the future of humanity. He is the crown of the new humanity. He pulls us forward to realize a greater share of that new humanity. He calls us out of our past and our natural beginnings; he delivers us in hope from the present and its critical failures. He drives us forward in mission, a universal mission to all men, not only to the few inside our borders, to the tribe that shares our color or the class that shares our customs, but to all men. No amount of patriotism or nationalism, whether your country is at war or peace, can cause you to deny the humanity of all the people whom God loves, for whom Christ died, and whom he represents as the advocate of their peace, freedom, unity, and fullness of life. Whether they will call you a good patriot or red-blooded countryman as you pursue this mission of Christ is hard to predict. Suffice it to remember that Jesus said, "They will put you out of the synagogues [or the churches] ; indeed, the hour is coming when whoever kills you will think he is offering a service to God" (John 16:2).

They will do that when you have to make a choice between the Mammon of your nation and the God of Abraham who said, "Go from your country . . . and I will make of you a blessing to all the nations of the earth." We are on the path of searching out these blessings.

24

Christianity
as Perpetual
Non-Conformity

Romans 12:2: "Do not be conformed to this world but be transformed by the renewal of your mind."

Luke 2:41-52: "Now his parents went to Jerusalem every year at the feast of the Passover. And when he was twelve years old, they went up according to custom; and when the feast was ended, as they were returning, the boy Jesus stayed behind in Jerusalem. His parents did not know it, but supposing him to be in the company they went a day's journey, and they sought him among their kinsfolk and acquaintances; and when they did not find him, they returned to Jerusalem, seeking him. After three days they found him in the temple, sitting among the teachers, listening to them and asking them questions; and all who heard him were amazed at his understanding and his answers. And when they saw him they were astonished; and his mother said to him, 'Son, why have you treated us so? Behold, your father and I have been looking for you anxiously.' And he said to them, 'How is it that you sought me? Did you not know that I must be in my Father's house?' And they did not understand the saying which he spoke to them. And he went down with them and came to Nazareth, and was obedient to them; and his mother kept all these things in her heart.

"And Jesus increased in wisdom and in stature, and in favor with God and man."

1. THE DEATH OF CONFORMIST CHRISTIANITY

As Christians we have just gone through a period in which Christianity was bowing and scraping before the god of this secular age. Christianity has become so secular that many of its dominant expressions neither excite nor offend. A lot of the Christianity we know is the gospel minus its stumbling block. In Christian theology we have seen a series of editions of secular Christianity; it is called "secular theology." The best seller of the sixties was *The Secular City.* This was meant to be the fulfillment of Dietrich Bonhoeffer's prophecy that the time was coming soon when there would be no religious people around anymore. If Christianity was to survive at all, it too would have to become radically secular. It would have to become nonreligious.

We have gone through a period in which Christianity was posturing before the world, imitating the world, transforming itself into a worldly phenomenon. Bonhoeffer's prophecy has come true, we have produced a secular Christianity. But our hearts are empty; our spirits are void. We have entered the valley of dry bones and we have seen Christians become secular skeletons without soul, without spirit.

Bonhoeffer was sitting in prison when he prophesied the coming of a man who would be utterly tough, worldly, and nonreligious, without any need for God, the church, or religious medicine. The man come of age, the secular man, was not a weakling falling to his knees, stretching out his hand for help, certainly not the kind of help the church could bring. When people read Bonhoeffer's prophecy, they fell for it. Christians tried to become the secular man. Bonhoeffer was a product of the Germany that produced Hitler. Bonhoeffer's picture of the secular man reflects elements of the infamous image of the Hitler youth — the radically secular man in a world come of age.

We have learned something from the phenomenon of secular Christianity, but now it is dying the death of pernicious anemia. St. Paul said, "Do not be conformed to this world." Secular Christianity was an accommodation to this world. One of its chief spokesmen said, "I am no longer religious. I am a secular man, and I want to understand Christianity in secular terms." The proposal was further refined and radicalized, until we heard that God was dead. Everything was dead. The church was dead. Worship was dead. The traditional symbols were dead. Nothing was alive except what was going on in the wonderful secular world. Secular Christianity has had the headlines for the last ten years, and now it is dying. It is falling into the grave that it dug for all its enemies.

Where does that leave us? We are now in the midst of a religious backlash. Religion is back in again. Someone has said, "There is a revival of religion everywhere — except in the church." A great part of the American church swallowed the wares hawked by the secular theologians and the secular ecclesiastical bureaucrats to make itself relevant. But it left the people inside the churches empty, and provided only amusement to the people outside.

We are now in the midst of a fantastic upsurge of interest in the religiously exotic. The other night we browsed our way through some of the book stores in Chicago's Old Town. The section is growing on eastern mysticism necromancy, witchcraft, magic, and astrology. I was surprised to see the same thing at Kroch's and Brentano's — an amazing collection of new books on weird forms of spirituality. We are supposed to be living in a secular age, and yet I read somewhere that there are over twent-five thousand practicing astrologists in America. What does it prove? Only that man cannot live on a diet of the secular alone. There is no deep satisfaction in the do-it-yourself religion of secular Christianity.

2. THE RENEWAL OF THE CHRISTIAN MIND

Secular Christianity was flying in the face of St. Paul's words, "Do not be conformed to the world." But Paul went on to say, "Be transformed by the renewal of your mind." This transformation is something vastly different from the rise of the new religiosity. For Christianity to jump now on the bandwagon of the new religiosity would only be another case of conforming to the world. The world has its own religions, its own brands of religiosity. It can swing back and forth between secularism and religiosity. With the return to religion we will be facing a new temptation, to convert Christianity into a religion again, into mere religiosity. What have we gained if we flip from a Christianity without religion only to flop into a religion without Christ?

The new religiosity is not the gospel of Jesus Christ. It is the law of God, bringing judgment without grace, revealing a sickness unto death. The new religiosity is a revolt. Paul Goodman, the late social critic, was right in seeing the new religiosity as a rebellion against the powers and principalities of our time, against the scientific dogmas, the technological controls, that place such a low ceiling on the quality of human life that the hunger for happiness and transcendence goes unsatisfied. People feel alienated in a world that does not grant the meaning they long for.

The new religiosity is, as Goodman says, a bunch of Luthers in search of a new reformation. It is a religious critique of the secular society. What is needed next is a conversion of the new religiosity. Christianity cannot live by the secular alone; neither can it coexist with a Christ-less religiosity. To be transformed by the renewal of our minds is a movement of spirit beyond the new religiosity. It is a response of faith to the manifestation of God's presence, the epiphany of his mystery in the person of Jesus. What needs to be utterly clear is that Christian faith is not merely a real groovy ethical life-style on the one hand, nor is it a lot of exotic religiosity on the other hand.

Christian faith is a specific response of one's mind and body to the appearance of Jesus of Nazareth in history. Transformation is conversion, getting one's head changed. This change comes about in response to what has appeared in Jesus. Already in the Gospel story of the twelve-year-old boy in the temple, there was occasion for amazement and astonishment. Jesus was sitting among his teachers, and they were amazed at his understanding and his answers.

I would like to stress a deceptively simple formula for keeping Christian faith on the beam, as we are tempted to oscillate wildly according to the spirit of the times, first becoming barrenly secular, then becoming weirdly religious. The formula is from Herbert Butterfield: "Hold to Jesus Christ, and for the rest be totally uncommitted." Whether we are more secular, or more religious, we are the Lord's; neither one has any advantage over the other. It is only a matter of psychological difference and preference. Some like it hot, some like it cold; some like the incense pot; some like the old-fashioned gospel songs; others can't stand either, but would rather carry a peace sign in front of the Pentagon. What is specifically of the Christian faith is a response to the wonder that has appeared in Jesus of Nazareth.

The astonishment of the people who encountered this twelve-year-old boy wonder in the temple was perhaps, first of all, just a response to the wonderful wisdom of a gifted child. Children can be full of wisdom anyway. "Out of the mouths of babes and sucklings, thou hast brought perfect praise." J. Robert Oppenheimer has said, "There are children playing in the street who could solve some of my top problems in physics, because they have the modes of sensory perception that I lost long ago."

Children can help us to gain a new sense of wonder. Jesus saw the quality of the kingdom in little children. "Unless you turn and become like children, you will never enter the kingdom of heaven." Jesus displayed this quality that day, listening — the quality of receptivity and asking questions — that is, the quality of curiosity. Children will have to help us to blow holes in our tightly enveloped world, to make room for new wonder, to see the world as a medium of mystery. The root problem of the drug culture is that young people are entering a wonderless world. They take off on a psychedelic quest for a chemical form of mysticism. Anything is better than a completely mastered world, the scent of incense or nonsense, mysticism or magic.

The epiphany of Jesus is not merely an example of the

wonder of childhood. It was a special case of a new consciousness. "I must be in my Father's house." His father and mother did not understand what that meant. But Mary kept the saying in her heart. This new consciousness in Jesus, already powerfully manifest in his childhood, is the source of the transformation that St. Paul is talking about. It's the source of the renewal of our minds.

This new consciousness is contagious; it is like something we catch. It is not an intellectual achievement. In fact, St. Paul said, it flies in the face of the wisdom of the wise; it conflicts with the understanding of the prudent. God has chosen the seemingly weak and childlike things of the world to confound the things that are mighty.

The figure of Jesus is still an amazing manifestation of God that arouses wonder and astonishment, surpassing all human understanding. The rock opera, *Jesus Christ Superstar*, has captured the quality of this amazement with sensitivity and reverence. A priest asks the question, "What are we to do about this *Jesusmania?*" People in the crowd are pressing hard for an answer to the concern. "Jesus Christ Superstar, tell us if you're who they say you are." "Jesus Christ Superstar, do *you* think you're what they say you are?" In another scene Jesus is standing before Herod, and Herod says, "I only ask things I'd ask any superstar. What is it you've got that puts you where you are?" The answer then is heard only in the ambiguous sounds of the hammer driving the nails through the hands of Jesus into the beams of the cross.

From the cross we hear the words of Jesus, spoken out of that same new amazing consciousness, the consciousness of Jesus in union with his Father. "Father, into your hands I commend my spirit." That is the faith of Jesus that becomes our faith in Jesus. Here is the one who knows the Father, the only begotten Son. Here is the one who can show us the Father, the source and the goal of our lives. Here is the One who can make all things new for us — giving us new values, new goals, a new vision, new freedom, and a new awareness. Here in Jesus is the appearance of the wondrously new reality that can deliver the church from its captivity to the secular spirit, and all its works and ways, the new reality that can lead the church beyond the temptation to fall into the new religiosity, with all its weird rituals of self-salvation. Faith in the wonder of God in the person of Jesus can gather up all that is good and acceptable in both the secular Christianity and the new religiosity to show forth what is the will of God for our time and the renewal of our church.